NEWBURY HOUSE SERIES:

INNOVATIONS IN FOREIGN LANGUAGE EDUCATION

HOWARD B. ALTMAN, Series Editor

To   W.H.F.,
      D.J.R.,
      L.B.R.

Preface

H. H. Stern
Director, Modern Language Center
Ontario Institute for Studies in Education

All language teaching inevitably, tacitly or openly, implies a theory of language and a theory of language learning. Every language teacher must somehow have an answer to two questions: What is the nature of language? And, what is the nature of the language learning process? It is therefore not surprising to find language teachers responsive to the disciplines which discuss such questions: linguistics and psychology above all, and more recently, psycholinguistics and sociolinguistics. But the relationship between the practice of language teaching and the underlying disciplines presents problems. If the language teacher makes himself impervious to the developments in the social sciences, he is out of touch with the advances of thought which change the intellectual climate in which we live. If he is too responsive, he may become confused or the victim of academic fashions. Psychologists and linguists have not always been too helpful. Sometimes they have given language teachers positive and sweeping advice in a dogmatic way; at other times, they have doggedly refused to draw the practical inferences of research, and sometimes they have paradoxically done both almost in the same breath.

Fortunately, there are a few scholars who have taken a sympathetic interest in the problems of second language teaching and who have interpreted their discipline to the language teaching profession, pointing out the more enduring advances and their possible relevance to language instruction. There are also a few language teachers who have looked critically at the research evidence and studied its practical implications. Perhaps scholars of the stature of J. B. Carroll illustrate well the former, whereas Wilga Rivers is a good example of the latter. It is by the intellectual integrity and the critical acumen of the individuals in these two categories that we are protected from working with outmoded conceptualizations, without falling into the trap of being pushed around by the winds of intellectual fashion.

It is therefore a pleasure and a great honor to be able to introduce the present volume of essays by Wilga Rivers.

Since 1964, when Dr. Rivers' first major work, *The Psychologist and the Foreign-Language Teacher* appeared and immediately made its impact, her influence has been considerable and, in my view, entirely beneficient. In the eight year period that has elapsed since then, through this first book as well as her second major work, *Teaching Foreign-Language Skills*, she has established herself as one of the foremost, if not *the* foremost methodologist, whose reputation is world-wide. She commands such a wide following because, while she has been responsive to the trends of thought in psychology and linguistics, she has never lost touch with the reality with which the classroom teacher has to deal. She has remained a language teacher, and teachers who hear her or read her writings immediately sense that what she says is tempered by practical experience and informed by abundant common sense.

These qualities are also evident in these essays, and, therefore, I find myself once more in sympathy with their general tenor. Just as in 1964 she warned us not to be silly about audiolingualism, today she warns us, very justifiably, and in a timely fashion, against superficial extrapolations from first language acquisition and transformational grammar, against simplistic interpretations of the cognitive approach, as well as against falling for the banal trappings of a hastily concocted individualization of instruction. At the same time, she indicates that there are areas of research in cognitive psychology which can indeed deepen our understanding of second language learning.

In the early sixties Wilga Rivers was foremost among those who protected language teaching from becoming trapped in the over-simplified psychology of learning which was current in much of the practice and theoretical expressions of the New Key or audiolingual approach. At that time she argued that the psychology of learning, as expressed by psychologists, was far more subtle and far more complex than was commonly recognized in language teaching theory. In the period between *The Psychologist and the Foreign-Language Teacher* and this volume, many of the assumptions of audiolingualism have been questioned. The New Key has become orthodox and traditional, and the modern linguist has to cope with a dubious new animal, a "new orthodoxy," to quote J. B. Carroll's phrase (1971), compounded from such descriptors as transformational grammar, first language acquisition, nativism, creativity, rationalism, cognitive code theory, and individualization. Wilga Rivers' present collection of papers does for the theories of 1972 what *The Psychologist and the Foreign-Language Teacher* did for the theory development of the early sixties.

In conclusion I would like to comment on two major tasks which seem to emerge from these essays.

The first task arises from the clash between audiolingualism and cognitive code theory. Audiolingualism has been associated with empiricism and structuralism in linguistics, and with behaviorism and learning theory in psychology; cognitive code theory has somehow come to be associated with transformational grammar and rationalism in linguistics, and with cognition and child language acquisition in psychology. The conflict has been unnecessarily sharpened into a struggle between two supposedly contrasting philosophies. I think it is the intention of Wilga Rivers in certain of these articles, just as it was the intention of J. B. Carroll in his TESOL address of 1971, to cut across these divisions by looking much more critically than is fashionable at present at the language teaching theory which claims to be based on

Chomsky's views, while suggesting other ways in which transformational theory may appropriately be applied. Such bridge building, as is exemplified by Carroll's notion of "cognitive habit-formation theory," or in Dr. Rivers' account of cognitive features in *all* second language learning regardless of school of thought is indeed salutary and timely. It is also useful to see some of the would-be profundities on the application of our *faculté de langage* to second language learning being cut down to size. Such discussions restore balance and lead to the expectation of what Carroll has called a meaningful synthesis.

A second task for a future language teaching theory, central to many of Wilga Rivers' observations, is to improve the relationship between language teaching practice and the disciplines, particularly psychology and linguistics. Like her, I believe that we cannot ignore the developments in the disciplines and must constantly examine changes in scientific thought and scholarship for their relevance to language teaching. We are therefore bound to scan psychological research and to make value judgements as to which area is promising or unpromising from the language teacher's point of view. But the kind of unsatisfactory dependence of language teaching theory on thought in other disciplines will prevail, as long as the psychology of second language learning is forced to rely on extrapolation from related fields and is not based on its own foundations.

I therefore wholeheartedly agree with Dr. Rivers when, at the beginning of her article entitled "The Foreign-Language Teacher and Cognitive Psychology or Where Do We Go from Here?," she invites teachers "to know as much as we possibly can about the way the student learns and learns language" (p. 73). Again, towards the end of this paper, quoting from John Dewey, she urges us to return to certain educational roots. This quotation together with a few remarks scattered throughout the paper suggest to me that she urges teachers to "think carefully about how students learn" (p. 89) and to make that the basis of language teaching.

What is needed in order to meet this demand are psychological and methodological studies of second language learning *per se*. It is my conviction that the psychology of second language learning has not yet received the treatment that it deserves. If we look at any book on psycholinguistics or on language acquisition, with very few exceptions (such as Ervin and Osgood, 1954),[1] second language learning simply is not represented or only marginally. What we have, therefore, are extrapolations or hypotheses derived from first language acquisition, first language use, bilingualism, verbal learning and verbal behavior, educational psychology, and the psychology of cognition. It is thus not surprising to find an element of uncertainty and puzzling discrepancies in the current treatment of psychological issues in second language teaching theory.

A psychology of second language learning in its own right will, of course, not isolate itself from other branches of psychology or from other disciplines for that matter. It will gain perspective by being related to other forms of code acquisition and code deficit. I hope that the study of second language learning processes will thus not only benefit language teaching but also contribute to the development of a broader theory of language acquisition and language use which will be derived from first *and* second language learning. Such studies will relate second language learning to many other phenomena: bilingualism and bidialectism, the learning of different codes or registers within one language and at different stages in life, and to the corresponding phenomena of code deficit and loss, such as deafness, aphasia, or stuttering.

While language teachers should press for such sorely needed direct research on the psychology of second language learning, we can hardly be expected to wait for such a long-term objective to be reached. Meanwhile we are grateful for guidance on existing research. No one has given us more discriminating and more practical help in making use of what is available in psychology than Wilga Rivers.

H. H. Stern
Toronto, August 1972

---

[1] S. M. Ervin and C. E. Osgood, "Second Language Learning and Bilingualism", in C. E. Osgood and T. A. Sebeok, *Psycholinguistics: A Survey of Theory and Research Problems* (Bloomington: Indiana University Press, 1954), pp. 139-45.

Contents

Introduction

A Personal Communication: From the Author to Her Reader

We often speak of language as a vehicle of expression—a metaphor which can illumine many aspects of our foreign-language teaching situation. In "Rules, Patterns, and Creativity" I speak of "a vehicle of meaning which (people) do not even realize they are using,"[1] in other words a vehicle which is transporting a person's message somewhere, but which itself is not the object of the trip. Before students can use such a vehicle for their purposes it must be constructed, and this construction demands a blueprint and various stages of production, with tryouts as the various sections and combinations are assembled—tryouts during which what has been assembled to date is used, if only momentarily, for its ultimate purpose. With our language vehicle this ultimate purpose is expression: a person revealing himself to, or disguising himself or hiding himself from, another or other persons. Expression involves all the problems of interpersonal relations. For this reason it is frequently less painful for teachers and students to continue working at the construction of the vehicle than to attempt to try it out for level of performance.

Here I would refer you to the model of foreign-language teaching set out in "Talking off the Tops of Their Heads",[2] where I distinguish skill-getting, represented by both *cognition* and *production* (or pseudocommunication), from

---

[1]See p. 12 of this book.

[2]See Article 2 in this book. The reader should familiarize himself with the full description of this model before proceeding.

skill-using in *interaction*, which involves both reception and expression and is dependent on motivation to communicate.

The construction of our vehicle presupposes a design. Some particularly talented individuals can put the design into effect without the help of the blueprint; they appear to move directly from model to production which means that they develop their own internal representation from acquaintance with the model. These are the exceptions, however. Most need help in developing a series of blueprints of increasing complexity as a basis for production. Some prefer lessons in drafting blueprints, others can draw them up from experience with a prototype of the vehicle. These blueprints are indicated in my model by the term *cognition* and they represent the system underlying both reception and expression. Our students depend on their blueprints as they put the parts together in *production* so that the vehicle will function. Sometimes students try merely to copy someone else's assembly. This may work for a time but leaves the student bewildered as the assembly becomes more complicated. At this stage only those with comprehensive blueprints, or internal representations, are able to make the mechanism operate as they would like. Construction is not, however, the use of the vehicle—this is represented by the trying-out that continually takes place as the assembly takes form. It is only through such tryouts that the operation of the vehicle can be smoothly integrated and faults corrected and the user gain confidence in handling it.

No analogy should be pushed too far. I have given attention to the differences between the blueprint, the assembly of the vehicle, and its trying out in use in "Rules, Patterns, and Creativity." In "Contrastive Linguistics in Textbook and Classroom" I have shown how knowledge of other blueprints (notably that of one's native language) can be a help only if the systematic nature of blueprints is fully understood and apparent similarities are viewed in relation to whole sections of the design. In "From Skill Acquisition to Language Control" I have reemphasized the fact that mere production of itself is not sufficient. In every lesson it must be regarded as preliminary to actual trying out of what is being learned so that from the earliest stages all learning activities lead to some form of real communication rather than remaining at the level of pseudocommunication through imposed utterances.

Interaction has always been the most neglected part of the essential language activities in our model. With the increasing trend toward individualization of instruction this situation will not be improved unless definite steps are taken to include substantial interaction activities in each program. A student alone with a book or tape, or both, is limited to cognition and production. Working with a few fellow students no more confident than himself on the usual type of program he still lacks the stimulus to use the foreign language for natural purposes. Interaction does not take place in a void. It is not enough to put several people together; there must also be some situational stimulus which naturally elicits an interchange. Interaction is a purposeful person to person affair in speech and in most kinds of writing. This interpersonal character of interaction explains why so much teaching and learning of foreign language remains at the production or pseudocommunication level.

In most classrooms there is very little reason or opportunity for students or teachers to reveal themselves to each other: the relationship is a formal and formalized one for which conventionalities suffice. The teacher is there to teach; the student is there to learn what the teacher or the administration thinks he should learn. The usual greetings are exchanged, conventional questions are asked about material presented aurally or graphically, conventional answers arising from the material are expected. Common remarks which may be heard are: "Come to the point, Johnny. We're not interested in your personal history;" "Don't ask silly questions;" "That's nothing to do with it. Didn't you hear the question?" John Holt describes for us the mechanisms students employ to defend themselves in class and protect their real selves from the humiliation and embarrassment which could result if they ventured to express themselves in an uncertain, often hostile environment[3] (and this in their

---

[3]John Holt, *How Children Fail* (New York: Dell, 1970). Originally published by Pitman, 1964.

native language). The psychological aspects of motivation to speak the language and suggestions for meaningful classroom activities are described in "Motivating through Classroom Techniques."

G. I. Brown points out that "attempts at communication solely on a rational level are bound to fail when the issues involved have personal relevance for the participants. Personal relevance connotes an affective dimension; people feel and value as well as think about the position they hold. Denying or ignoring the existence of feelings in communication is like building a house without a foundation or framework."[4] No wonder it is more comfortable for student and teacher in the foreign-language class to remain at the level of pseudocommunication. Those who advocate that foreign-language instruction should begin with spontaneous communication and free interaction without any preparation with structured materials are ignoring this affective element.

Spontaneous communication and free interaction are possible in any language only when teachers and their students have built up a warm, uninhibited, confident, sympathetic relationship and when such a relationship also exists among the students themselves. In the first lessons no such state of affairs exists as yet. The teacher's efforts from the beginning should be devoted to building up such relationships through enjoyable, successful experiences in using interesting and amusing segments of language in a multiplicity of ways so that the student begins to feel that he can express real concerns through this new medium and that it is exhilarating to do so. This confident attitude, so essential to development of future speaking skill, is very fragile and can be stifled quite early by a situation where the teacher has the advantage of fluency and is inevitably right while the student is uncertain, groping, and for the most part wrong. Early interaction practice calls for self-restraint and tact on the part of the teacher. Once the students understand the rules of the game—that you do the most you can with the little you have in some meaningful activity shared with others

---

[4]George Issac Brown, *Human Teaching for Human Learning: an Introduction to Confluent Education* (New York: Viking Press, 1971), p. 6.

in the group, and that the teacher is there not to condemn but to give a helping hand, a gentle reminder, and much encouragement—confident self-expression is possible even at a very early stage. The types of activities which can be used to give purpose to interaction practice are set out in "Talking off the Tops of Their Heads."

It is because of this fundamental interpersonal factor that methods and techniques imposed on the teacher, efficient as they might have seemed in the abstract in terms of language-learning theory, have always proved successful for some people working with some classes but not for all. The interaction of teacher personality, multiple student person-alities, and what each brings into the classroom from the outside can be observed only in unique situations. Take away one student from the group or add one student and you immediately have a new mix. Change the teacher and the situation is no longer the same. All teachers are conscious of this fact which has been the bane of large-scale investigations and experimentation in teaching method.

Is methodology then futile? Not at all. Methodology should be based on what we know about language (what it is and how it operates—still a matter of controversy); what we know about human beings (how they learn and how they learn language and whether these are different processes or merely different manifestations of the same process—another question which is still under investigation); and what we know about people in interaction (a prolific area of psychological study). It is inevitable, then, that method-ological recommendations will change as our knowledge of these three factors evolves, with earlier postulates being rejected and new premises accepted. Teachers should keep in touch with findings in these areas and share the excitement of a developing and progressing discipline. "The Foreign-Language Teacher and Cognitive Psychology or Where Do We Go from Here?" and "Linguistic and Psychological Factors in Speech Perception and Their Implications for Teaching Materials" will supply teachers with much new information, particularly in the psychology of perception.

At this point the teacher takes over as a professional person and as an individual with his own gifts, insights, and preferences. First, he must know himself and his strengths and weaknesses in interpersonal relations. Then he must know his students: who they are, what their aspirations are, and how they learn as individuals. He will find that their general attitudes fluctuate, not only from generation to generation or from decade to decade but, in this period of rapid change, almost from year to year. (The attitudes of the present generation are discussed in relation to foreign-language programs in "Foreign Languages in a Time of Change.") Senior high school students may still accept what their younger brothers and sisters are already rejecting. In the early sixties, for instance, with a more docile student population, it seemed possible to subordinate the individual to the efficient system for his own good, as seen by his teachers; now the efficient system must be subordinated to individual learning preferences if there is to be a high quality of learning. This is a period of plurality of objectives and diversity of learning approaches, a subject I discuss in "From the Pyramid to the Commune: the Evolution of the Foreign-Language Department." The teacher in this volatile period must understand how teaching and learning relate to each other and interact fruitfully, realizing that either can exist without the other. He must learn to teach in such a way that he does not interpose himself between the learner and what is to be learned. He must accept and encourage a variety of learning styles allowing for differences in individuals. Some learn more by the ear than the eye, others learn through printed texts; some learn through abstract reflection, some through concrete manipulation; some learn more slowly than others; some prefer to learn by themselves, while others prefer help, even direction, and need the stimulation of a group if they are to realize their potentialities. The foreign-language teacher for this generation must expect and respect a new clientele and study how he can devise a learning program for students of a type to which he was not accustomed before. These and related matters are examined in "Teacher-Student Relations: Coercion or Cooperation?"

By this time the teacher's head is spinning, maybe. He has listened, he has studied, he has read. None of this is sufficient. The truly successful teacher is highly idiosyncratic.

From this plethora of information and recommendations, he selects. He takes from the new what suits his own personality and his teaching style and what is appropriate for the personalities and aspirations of his own students, thus forming his own approach. He is not afraid to innovate, to rearrange, to redesign his courses, because continual reflection and appropriate adjustment and readjustment keep him professionally alive, making him a more interesting person to his students. Above all, he does not remain caught up in his own discipline but sees it in relation to the total educational experience. He sees himself contributing, along with his colleagues in mathematics, in social studies, in guidance, to the maturation process of young minds and personalities. He remains in step with changing approaches to the whole curriculum and views his subject in that perspective. In step? Why should he not be in the vanguard in meeting new challenges and seeking new opportunities?

So we move, let us hope, as a profession into an era of tolerance and acceptance of difference—the era of the commune, where divisive and acrimonious competition to draw teachers in one direction and then in another will appear irrelevant, and the word "best" will be recognized for the subjective and relative term that it is. Let us look forward to a period of "many flowers blooming, daylilies perhaps, but each in its day and hour bringing fragrance to the experience of some."[5] Invite me to visit your garden at that stage so that I can see what your skill and care have brought into being.

Wilga M. Rivers

Urbana-Champaign,
June, 1972

---

[5]See p. 125 of this book.

1

Rules, Patterns, and Creativity[*]

In 1966, Chomsky shocked many participants at the Northeast Conference by casting doubt on the validity of the direct and uncritical application of linguistic theory to teaching practice. "I am, frankly," he said, "rather skeptical about the significance, for the teaching of languages, of such insights and understanding as have been attained in linguistics and psychology."[1] "It is possible—even likely—" he continued, "that principles of psychology and linguistics, and research in these disciplines, may supply insights useful to the language teacher. But this must be demonstrated and cannot be presumed. It is the language teacher himself who must validate or refute any specific proposal."[2]

With an obvious, though unstated, reference to methods of foreign-language teaching of recent years which it had been believed were consistent with what was known of the nature of language and of the learning process, Chomsky declared: "Linguists have had their share in perpetuating the myth that linguistic behavior is 'habitual' and that a fixed stock of 'patterns' is acquired through practice and used as the basis for 'analogy'."[3] To Chomsky, "Language is not a 'habit-structure.' Ordinary linguistic behavior characteristically involves innovation, formation of new sentences and new patterns in accordance with rules of great abstractness and intricacy."[4] For this reason, he speaks continually of the " 'creative' aspect of language use."[5]

---

[*] This is a revised version of an article, "Grammar in Foreign Language Teaching," which appeared in the *Modern Language Journal* 52 (1968), 206-11.

Linguistic science has made teachers very conscious of the fact that grammar is the core of language. Without an internalized set of rules, or syntax, they are told, no one can understand or use a language: language is "rule-governed behavior."[6] In the past, many teachers have uncritically adopted habit-formation techniques because language, it appeared, was "a set of habits."[7] Now many are ready to seize upon a new slogan and begin to inculcate rules in the hope of establishing "rule-governed behavior," even though they have only a vague concept of what this phrase can mean as it has been used by linguists or psychologists.[8] In this way they hope to take their students beyond the arid fields of mechanical repetition, where pure habit-formation techniques seem so often to have left them, into the greener pastures of creative production of foreign-language utterances.

Before we decide on any particular approach, we need to clarify our ideas about the essence of language use (which in Chomsky's terms is a question of performance based on competence). We will then select methods appropriate to the type of learning involved in its effective acquisition. It is at this point that there is most confusion.

Linguistic vs. Pedagogic Grammar

First, it is important to distinguish, as Chomsky has done in *Topics in the Theory of Generative Grammar*, between a linguistic and a pedagogic grammar. A linguistic grammar, as Chomsky sees it, aims to discover and exhibit the mechanisms that make it possible for a "speaker to understand an arbitrary sentence on a given occasion," whereas a pedagogic grammar attempts to provide the student with the ability to understand and produce such sentences.[9]

This leaves the question wide open for the foreign-language teacher. A linguistic grammar is an account of competence (the knowledge of the language system that a native speaker has acquired) expressed in terms of an abstract model that does not necessarily represent, and may not even attempt to parallel, the psychological processes of language use. It can give the informed teacher insights into language structure and clarify for him various aspects of his subject matter, but methods of linguistic description do not *per se* provide any guidance as to how a student may learn to communicate in a foreign language. This is the preoccupation of the writer of a pedagogic grammar who, in the light of what the linguistic grammar has established about the subject matter, decides what are psychologically (and therefore pedagogically) the most appropriate ways of arranging and presenting the material to the students. The form a particular pedagogic grammar will assume will depend on such factors as the objectives of the language course (which devolve from the felt needs of the students), the age and intellectual maturity of the students, the length and intensity of the study, and the degree of contrast between the foreign and native languages.

How, then, can the foreign-language teacher establish "rule-governed behavior" that will enable his students to produce novel utterances at will? In conformity with Chomsky's position, we need to make it possible for the foreign-language learner to internalize a system of rules that can generate an infinite number of grammatical sentences that will be comprehensible and acceptable when uttered with the semantic and phonological components appropriate to specific communication situations.[10] With the word *internalize* we are at the heart of the problem: *"rule-governed behavior" in the sense in which it is used by linguists or psychologists does not mean behavior that results from the conscious application of rules.*

According to Chomsky, "A person is not generally aware of the rules that govern sentence-interpretation in the language that he knows; nor, in fact, is there any reason to suppose that the rules can be brought to consciousness." Neither can we "expect him to be fully aware even of the empirical consequences of these internalized rules"[11] —that is, of the way in which abstract rules acquire semantic interpretations. The behavior is "rule-governed" in the sense that it conforms to the internalized system of rules. These rules are not the pedagogic "grammar rules" (often of doubtful linguistic validity) of the traditional deductive, expository type of language teaching, according to which students docilely constructed language sequences. They are rules, as Chomsky puts it, of "great abstractness and intricacy" inherent in the structure of a language, which through the operation of various processes find expression in the overt forms that people produce.

Generate, in the mathematical sense in which Chomsky uses the term, does not refer to some unexpected production of language sequences that reflects originality of thought on the part of the speaker, but to a mechanical process: the outworking of the internalized rules will automatically result in what are recognizably grammatical utterances. When Chomsky talks, therefore, about the " 'creative' aspect of language use," he is not referring to that type of free play with language elements where students, with glib abandon, "create language," grammatical or ungrammatical, to suit their immediate purposes. He is referring to the fact that once the system of rules of the language has become an integral part of the student's store of knowledge he will be able to produce, in order to express his meaning, an infinite variety of language sequences, whether he has previously heard such sequences or not—sequences which are grammatically acceptable, and therefore comprehensible, to the person to whom he is speaking. The mere supplying of rules and training of the students in their use for the construction of language sequences is not in itself sufficient to ensure the "internalizing" of the system of rules so that it will operate in the production of sentences without the students being conscious of its role. Unless foreign-language teachers are aware of the technical meaning of the terms Chomsky was using in his speech on language teaching, they may be left with erroneous impressions of his viewpoint.

Creative Use of Language

Exercising the language teacher's prerogative that Chomsky has so clearly assigned us, we may well question his statement that it is a myth that linguistic behavior is "habitual" and that a fixed stock of patterns is acquired through practice and used as the basis for "analogy."[12] "Repetition of fixed phrases," he says, "is a rarity," and "it is only under exceptional and quite uninteresting circumstances that one can seriously consider how 'situational context' determines what is said."[13] Despite these assertions, Chomsky himself would be the first to admit that a theory of language performance has yet to be developed. With his continual emphasis on creative and innovative use of language,[14] Chomsky is likely to lead us astray in the teaching of foreign languages by fixing our attention on a distant rather than an immediate goal. It is certainly true that our final aim is to produce students who can communicate about anything and everything in the foreign language, creating at will novel utterances that conform to the grammatical system of the language, but, as in every other area of teaching, we must map out our program step by step.

Creative and innovative use of language still takes place within a restricted framework, a finite set of formal arrangements to which the speaker's utterances must conform if he is to be comprehended and thus to communicate effectively.[15] The speaker cannot "create" the grammar of the language as he innovates: he is making "infinite use of finite means."[16] His innovative ability will exist only to the degree that underlying competence exists—that the set of rules has been internalized. Foreign-language students must acquire the grammar of the foreign language so that it functions for them as does the grammar of their native language: as a vehicle of meaning that they do not even realize they are using.

Basically, the question of how to inculcate the grammar of a language will depend on the type of activity we believe communication in a foreign language to be: is it a skill or an intellectual process, or is it a blend of the two? If foreign-language learning is the acquiring of a skill or a group of interrelated skills, then our students need intensive practice until they are able to associate without hesitation or reflection the many linguistic elements that are interrelated in a linear sequence. If, on the other hand, foreign-language use is an intellectual process, then training is necessary to ensure that students can make correct choices of rules and modification of rules in order to construct utterances that express their intentions.

Two Levels of Language Behavior

If we can identify two levels of foreign-language behavior for which our students must be trained, then it is clear that one type of teaching will not be sufficient for the task. These two levels may be designated: (1) the level of *manipulation* of language elements that occur in fixed relationships in clearly defined closed systems (that is, relationships that will vary within very narrow limits), and (2) a level of *expression of personal meaning* at which possible variations are infinite, depending on such factors as the type of message to be communicated, the situation in which the utterance takes place, the relationship between speaker and hearer or hearers, and the degree of intensity with which the message is conveyed. If we recognize two such levels a place must be found for the firm establishment of certain basic linguistic habits and the understanding of a complex system with its infinite possibilities of expression. The problem is to define the role of each of these types of learning and their interrelationships in the acquiring of a foreign language.[17]

It is essential to recognize first that certain elements of language remain in fixed relationships in small, closed systems, so that once the system is invoked in a particular way a succession of interrelated formal features appears. Fluent speakers are able to make these interrelated adjustments irrespective of the particular message they wish to produce. The elements that interact in restricted systems may be practiced intensively in order to forge strong habitual associations from which the speaker never deviates (this applies to such elements as inflection of person and number, agreements of gender, fixed forms for interrogation or negation, formal features of tenses). These elements do not require intellectual analysis: they exist, and they must be used in a certain way in certain environments and in no other way.[18] For these features, intensive practice exercises of various kinds can be very effective learning procedures, with the teacher supplying a brief word of explanation where necessary to forestall hesitation or bewilderment. (Lengthy explanations can be a hindrance rather than a help for this type of activity because it is *how* these systems operate that matters, not *why*.)

Practice of this type should not be given in solid, tedious blocks in a determined attempt to stamp in these formal features once and for all. Shorter exercises reintroduced at intervals over a period of time, with interspersed opportunities to use these features in association with other language elements in a communicative interchange, no matter how simple, will be more effective in establishing the necessary control. In this way, the attention of the students will be more directly focussed in subsequent practice on areas which they have found to be of persistent difficulty. Structural practice of this type can be considered effective only if these formal features become readily available to the student when his attention is concentrated on constructing a message—an act which involves the second level of language behavior. They will not become readily available unless the student has early and constant practice in expressing his personal meaning.

At the second level, decisions more intimately connected with contextual meaning may bring into play any of a variety of syntactic structures, so that students will be continually reusing what they have learned. A decision at this higher level has structural implications beyond the word or the phrase, often beyond the sentence. A slight variation in the decision will often mean the construction of quite a different form of utterance. Naturally, then, decisions at the second level involve a more complicated initial choice, which entails further choices of a more limited character. In order to express exactly what one wishes to say, one must view it in relation to the potential of the structural system of the language as a whole and select accordingly. This is the higher-level decision that sets in motion operations at lower levels that are interdependent. The decision to make a particular type of statement about something that has taken place recently involves a choice of register, a choice of degree of intensity, the use of lexical items in certain syntactical relationships that will involve the production of certain morphological elements, certain phonemic distinctions, and certain stress and intonation patterns. The interrelationships within the language system that are involved in these higher-level decisions often need to be clarified in deductive fashion by the teacher or textbook. For effective practice at this level the student must understand the implications and ramifications of changes he is making. This he will best do if the practice involves making decisions in real communication situations devised in the classroom, rather than in artificial drills and exercises. In such interchanges the feedback from the other participants in communication brings a realization of the effect of the decisions the speaker has made.

There must be in the classroom, then, a constant interplay of learning by analogy and by analysis, of inductive and deductive processes—according to the nature of the operation the student is learning. It is evident that he cannot put higher-level choices into operation with ease if he has not developed facility in the production of the interdependent lower-level elements, and so learning by intensive practice and analogy have their place. Genuine freedom in language use, however, will develop only as the student gains control of the system as a whole, beyond the mastery of patterns in isolation. This control will become established only through much experience in attempting to counterbalance and interrelate various syntactic possibilities in order to convey a comprehensible meaning in a situation where its expression has some real significance.

It becomes clear that the second level of language use, which we have just considered, is of a more sophisticated type than the first level. It demands of the student understanding of the interrelationships and options the language system allows. This understanding guides his higher-level choices, yet full comprehensibility depends on his skill in manipulation of the numerous lower-level elements which are set in operation by the higher-level decisions. Too often in the past, foreign-language teaching concentrated on an understanding of the language system as a whole without providing sufficient practice in rapid production of the lower-level elements. This led to hesitancy in language use. On the other hand, more recent methods have worked out techniques for developing the lower-level manipulative skill while leaving the student unpracticed in the making of decisions at the higher level. The language course must provide for training at both levels.

It would be a mistake, however, to believe that practice at the second level should be delayed until the student has learned all the common features of the manipulative type—that is, that the student should first learn to manipulate elements in fixed relationships and not begin until a year or two later to learn the selection process of the higher level. If he is eventually to understand a complex system with its infinite possibilities of expression, he must develop this understanding little by little. The student will learn to make higher-level selective decisions by being made aware at every step of the meaningful use in communication of operations he is learning at the manipulative level. No matter how simple the pattern he is practicing, he will become aware of its possibilities for communication[19] when he attempts to use it for his own purposes and not just to complete an exercise or to perform well in a drill.

As each structure becomes a medium of communication, it takes its place in the evolving system of meaningful expression that the student is internalizing; by using it in relationship with what he has already learned, he sees this isolated operation as part of a whole, with a definite function within the language. As he acquires more knowledge of the language, he will need further explanation of how the various elements he has become accustomed to using interact within sentences and discourse. Such explanations will be brief and to the point. Since their sole purpose is to prevent mislearning through mistaken assumptions about relationships, they will be fruitful only if followed immediately by meaningful practice in the expression of these relationships. Such practice is essential until it is evident that the student has internalized the underlying rules so effectively that they govern his production without conscious and deliberate application on his part.

Whether at the first or second level, practice does not have to be boring and meaningless. It can take the form of games and competitions which call for the production of the types of structures being learned or conversational interchanges within a directional framework.[20] With a little thought, the classroom teacher can find interesting, even exciting ways to practice all kinds of structural combinations and inter-relationships until the student acquires confidence and assurance in their potentialities of expression.

As a further step, and this will be sooner or later according to the age and maturity of the class, the student will need to see the parts and the interacting sections he has learned in relation to the whole functioning system of the language. (Having learned, for instance, different ways of expressing past action, he will need to see how the past fits into the general expression of temporal relationships in this particular language.) In most cases, he will have had more practice in those areas where the danger of native-language interference is the greatest (that is, where the native and foreign languages are most divergent in their usage). At this advanced stage, the student will need to grasp, to understand, without referring to an external and therefore irrelevant criterion,[21] how apparent similarities and differences interact within the complete system of the language he is learning.

But let me emphasize again that the student cannot realize this understanding of the whole before he has experienced, through practice and active use, the functioning of the parts. If he attempts to possess the whole too soon, he will achieve only rote learning of grammar rules and the ability to describe rather than to use the grammatical system. On the other hand, where the teacher can present the system as a whole to students who already have a practical knowledge of the functioning of the parts, he can freely use all kinds of authentic language material, aural and graphic, to demon-strate what he wishes to convey. And by showing how the grammatical system works for real purposes the teacher can convey far more to the students than he can by making numerous abstract explanations supported by isolated, out-of-context examples.

Textbooks and courses of study—and teachers—must make ample provision at appropriate stages for both types of learning discussed here. Neglect of the practice needed to acquire such things as interrelated inflectional systems will force students to make decisions for each element as they proceed, and their use of the language will remain hesitant. On the other hand, it is only by going beyond the practice stage and trying out what they know in communication that students can learn to make the higher-level choices that will bring the lower-level adjustments they have learned into operation at the appropriate moment.

There has been much experimentation in recent years with techniques for the lower-level manipulative operations. We need now to give more thought to effective ways of inducing language behavior at the second level. The learner will understandably take his cue from his teacher. He will see that the use of what he is learning in spontaneous production is his most important task only when his teacher is convinced and convinces him that this is so, and when every exercise and classroom activity leads frankly and naturally to a further opportunity for personal expression in the language. It is often easier for teacher and students to keep on working at a manipulative level, finding immediate satisfaction in the mastery of small elements. The necessary and eagerly anticipated liberation in foreign-language use, however, will not occur unless concentrated effort is directed at all stages toward this very end.

FOOTNOTES

[1] Noam Chomsky, "Linguistic Theory," *Language Teaching: Broader Contexts*, ed. R. G. Mead, Jr., Report of Northeast Conference on the Teaching of Foreign Languages (New York: MLA Materials Center, 1966), p. 43.

[2] Ibid., p. 45.

[3] Ibid., p. 44.

[4] Ibid., p. 44.

[5] Ibid., p. 44.

[6]S. Saporta uses this term in "Applied Linguistics and Generative Grammar" in *Trends in Language Teaching*, ed. A. Valdman (New York: McGraw-Hill, 1966), p. 86.

[7]William G. Moulton, "Linguistics and Language Teaching in the United States 1940-1960," in *Trends in European and American Linguistics*, eds. C. Mohrmann, A. Sommerfelt, and J. Whatmough (Utrecht: Spectrum, 1961), p. 87.

[8]George A. Miller, "Some Preliminaries to Psycholinguistics," *American Psychologist*, 20 (1965):15-20. Reprinted in L. A. Jakobovits and M. S. Miron, eds., *Readings in the Psychology of Language* (Englewood Cliffs, New Jersey: Prentice-Hall, 1967), pp. 172-79; see especially p. 175.

[9]Noam Chomsky, *Topics in the Theory of Generative Grammar* (The Hague: Mouton, 1966), p. 10.

[10]Ibid., p. 16

[11]Ibid., p. 10.

[12]N. Chomsky, "Linguistic Theory," p. 44.

[13]Ibid., p. 46.

[14]Ibid., p. 44.

[15]J. B. Carroll in "Current Issues in Psycholinguistics and Second Language Teaching," *TESOL Quarterly* 5(1971):103, comments on Chomsky's position as follows: "I do not find any basic opposition between conceiving of language behavior as resulting from the operation of 'habits' and conceiving of it as 'rule-governed' . . . I would define a habit as any learned disposition to perceive, behave, or perform in a certain manner under specified circumstances. To the extent that an individual's language behavior conforms to the habits of the speech community of which he is a member, we can say that his behavior is 'rule-governed'."

[16]Chomsky, quoting Humboldt, in *Aspects of the Theory of Syntax* (Cambridge: MIT Press, 1965), p. 8.

[17]This subject is discussed in relation to all four fundamental language skills in Wilga M. Rivers, *Teaching Foreign-Language Skills* (Chicago: University of Chicago Press, 1968).

[18]It is interesting to note that many of these features, particularly the morphological ones, are excluded by Chomsky from his system of rewrite rules and included in the lexicon as parts of complex symbols. See *Aspects*, pp. 82-88.

[19]Ways of providing such practice are described in "Talking off the Tops of Their Heads," Article 2 in this book.

[20]A directional framework is provided unobtrusively when a discussion is set in motion which requires, for instance, conditional statements: "If you were (the Mayor), what would you (do?)" or past tense situations such as: "When I (came in), were you (talking)?" or "When you were (a baby), did you (cry) often?"

[21]The importance of understanding the operation of the target language as a system is discussed at greater length in "Contrastive Linguistics in Textbook and Classroom," Article 3 in this book.

2

Talking off the Tops of Their Heads[*]

In a description of the Defense Language Institute program I read: "After basic patterns and structures are mastered, the student can proceed to more and more controlled substitution and eventually to free conversation." How delightfully simple it sounds! We breathe the fresh air of the uncomplicated. The student "masters the basic patterns and structures," we provide him with carefully controlled practice, and hey presto! he speaks freely in unstructured situations.

There were times, in days which seem now to belong to another age, when faith in the efficacy of structured courses and controlled drills to produce fluent speakers of another language went unchallenged. We knew where we wanted to go; we knew how to get there; we were happy with our products—or were we? And were they? Are such cries of frustration as: "I can't say anything off the top of my head, it all comes out as phrases from the book" new to our ears?[1] This student complaint of the seventies sounds almost like a paraphrase of the more academic remark of 1948 that "while many students could participate in memorized conversations speedily and effortlessly, hardly any could produce at length fluent variations from the basic material, and none could talk

*Paper delivered at the Defense Language Institute English Language Branch, Lackland Air Force Base, Texas, on June 30, 1971, (TESOL Project). Originally published in *TESOL Quarterly,* 6 (1972), 71-81.

on unrehearsed topics without constant and painful hesitation."[2] In almost a quarter of a century we have still not come to grips with our basic problem: "How do we develop communicative ability in a foreign language?"[3] We may intensify practice in the classroom (practice of patterns, practice of variations of patterns, practice in selection of patterns), but how do we engineer the great leap? A child learns all kinds of swimming movements while his loving parent holds him, lets him go a little but is there to support him as he loses confidence; then at some moment he swims. One moment he is a nonswimmer, then he is a swimmer. The movements are the same, the activity is of a new kind—the difference is psychological. How does the nonswimmer become a swimmer? He becomes autonomous in his movements and in his directions: he draws on his own resources; he ceases to rely on somebody else's support; he takes off and he is swimming. How do we get our students to this autonomous stage of language use? This is the crucial point of our teaching. Until we have solved this problem we will continue to mark time: developing more and more efficient techniques for producing foreign language cripples, with all the necessary muscles and sinews but unable to walk alone. "Spontaneous expression," "liberated expression," "creative language use"—the terms may vary with changing emphases in our profession: the goal still eludes us. Let's see what we can do here and now to attack this problem in a direct and practical fashion.

We must examine the problem at the point at which we are stalled. How can we help the student pass from the storing of linguistic knowledge and information about how this knowledge operates in communication to actual using of this knowledge for the multitudinous, unpredictable purposes of an individual in contact with other individuals? We do not need new ways to help the student acquire linguistic knowledge—we know of many from our "twenty-five centuries of language teaching"[4] and each in its heyday has seemed to be effective for this purpose. Here we can pick and choose according to our theoretical persuasion, our temperamental preferences, and our assessment of the learning styles of the particular groups of students with whom we are dealing. In any case, these students will learn according to their personal strategies in the ultimate secret of their individual personalities, even when they appear to be doing as we direct.

We need a new model of our language teaching activity which allocates a full role to the student's individual learning in communication. I propose the following division of essential processes.

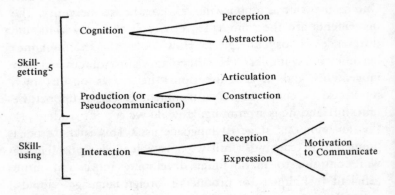

Ability to communicate, to interact verbally, presumes some knowledge (*cognition*) both in the perception of units, categories, and functions, and in the internalizing of the rules relating these categories and functions. I am not concerned here with how this knowledge is acquired and am willing to concede the validity (and probably the necessity) of a variety of approaches to such acquisitions. This knowledge must, however, be acquired. In the process of acquisition the student learns the *production* of language sequences: he learns through doing. Whether we use the terms "exercises" or "drills" or "activities" is immaterial; some kind of practice in putting together smoothly and confidently what he is learning is also essential. The student must learn to articulate acceptably and to construct comprehensible foreign-language sequences by rapid associations of learned elements. No matter how much we relate these activities to real-life situations this practice rarely passes beyond *pseudo-communication*. It is externally directed, not self-originating;

it is a dependent, not an independent, activity. The utterances may even be original in their combinations of segments but the student is not communicating anything that is of real import to him nor receiving any genuine message. This is practice in formulating communications and as such it is valuable practice. It is near-communication with all the outward appearances of communication, but the student does not have to demonstrate in these activities that he has taken the great leap into autonomy: the leap that is crucial. Our failure in the past has been in our satisfaction with students who perform well in pseudocommunication. We have tended to assume that there will then be automatic transfer to performance in *interaction*. We may have encouraged some sketchy attempts at autonomous inter- action, but always with the supporting hand: the instructor or the native speaker leading the group, drawing the student out, directing the interchange.

David Wolfe suggests that progress toward autonomy is hindered by the artificiality of language learning through "drills and exercises which force the student to lie. . . . From the point of view of true linguistic communication," he says, such "seemingly harmless sentences" as *Yesterday I went to the movies, Last night I went to the game, Last week I went to the game* "border on the nonsensical."[6] I do not think that this is the problem. We may maintain that lying is a form of real communication, but, this aspect aside, sentences in drills of this type are pseudocommunication in any case, and it may be clearer to students that this is so if they are sometimes also absurd. In a recent foreign-language text coauthored by the playwright Ionesco, the nonsensical and even whimsical approach to adult learning is purposefully exploited with students playing manipulatively with such sentences as "The teacher is in the pocket of the vest of the watch," "The crocodile is more beautiful than Mary-Jane," and "He says his parents are as big as the Eiffel Tower."[7] Such manipulations are intended to force students to think of the meaning of what they are saying which is one step toward autonomy, and pure nonsense may on occasions be more effective in this regard than the colorless, socially correct actions of Dick and Jane, of Maria and Pedro.

In recent writings on foreign-language teaching there has been increasing emphasis on communication, and on what are being called communication drills. I myself have spoken elsewhere of the necessity for relating the content of drills to the student's own interests: "Participation in the drill can be innovative: providing for practice in the repetition and variation of language segments, but with simultaneous practice in selection, as the student expresses his own meaning and not that of the textbook writer. . . . Practice in selection should not be considered a separate activity for advanced classes: it can and should be included in class work from the very first lessons."[8] "Many drills may be given the appearance of a game, or of elementary communication, by provoking the students into asking the teacher a series of questions in response to cues, or into making a series of comments about the teacher's activities and interests, or those of other students. The more the student is interested in an activity in the foreign language, the more he feels the desire to communicate in the language, and this is the first and most vital step in learning to use language forms spontaneously."[9]

Christina Paulston has developed the communication drill concept in more detail.[10] She groups drills into mechanical drills, meaningful drills, and communicative drills. In mechanical drills, there is complete control of the response so that the student does not even need to understand the drill to produce the correct response (as in simple substitution drills). Paulston suggests that if a nonsense word can be inserted as effectively by the student as a meaningful word, then the drill is of the mechanical type. This is pure production: sometimes merely practice in articulation, at other times practice in constructing an orderly sequence. As such it has its place in the initial phase of introducing a new structure or for practicing some problem of pronunciation or intonation. An example of such a drill would be:

> Pattern: I'm reading a book.
> Cue: Magazine.
> Response: I'm reading a magazine.

Cue: Newspaper.
Response: I'm reading a newspaper.

In meaningful drills "there is still control of the response (although it may be correctly expressed in more than one way ...) but the student cannot complete the drill without fully understanding structurally and semantically what he is saying." The following would be a meaningful drill:

Question: When did you arrive this morning?
Answer: I arrived at nine o'clock.
Question: When will you leave this evening?
Answer: I'll leave at six o'clock.

In a communicative drill, however, "there is no control of the response. The student has free choice of answer, and the criterion of selection here is his own opinion of the real world—whatever he wants to say." This sounds like autonomous interaction, but Paulston continues: "Whatever control there is lies in the stimulus. . . .It still remains a drill rather than free communication because we are still within the realm of the cue-response pattern." She gives the example: "What did you have for breakfast?" with its possibility of an orthodox response such as "I had toast and coffee for breakfast," or the unorthodox "I overslept and skipped breakfast so I wouldn't miss the bus." It is clear that the unconventional student may well turn this into real interaction, but my guess is that the majority of students, feeling insecure in their knowledge of the language, would remain in the area of pseudocommunication.

Adrian Palmer suggests what he calls "communication practice drills."[11] "In communication practice (CP) drills, the student finds pleasure in a response that is not only linguistically acceptable, but also conveys information personally relevant to himself and other people." As outlined, this is an interesting technique. Palmer maintains that "the most powerful technique at the teacher's disposal is his ability to verbally create situations which could be relevant to the student's own life and then to force the student to think about the meaning and consequences of what he would say in such situations." His CP drills are drills in that they center around practice of particular structures such as:

I would tell him   to   shut the door
*　　　　　her　　　　turn on the light*
*　　　　　them　　　bring some food*

He develops them, however, by a somewhat Socratic method:

"Teacher: 'Karen, if you and Susan came to class
　　　　　　at 8 a.m. and it was winter and the room
　　　　　　was dark at 8 a.m., what would you tell
　　　　　　Susan?'

Karen: (with any luck at all) 'I would tell
　　　　　　her to turn on the light.'

Teacher: 'And how about you, Paul, if you were
　　　　　　with Mary and you wanted to read, what
　　　　　　would you do?'

Paul: 'I would tell her to turn on the light.'

Teacher: (in student's native language) 'You
　　　　　　as a boy would tell a girl to do that for you?'

Teacher: (continuing in the target language)
　　　　　　'Paul, if you came alone, and if I was in
　　　　　　the room, what would you do?'

Paul: 'I would tell you to turn on the light.'

Teacher: 'Then I would throw you out of class.' "

In this type of drill Palmer is moving toward interaction in that a student who gives mechanically what appears to be a correct response may well be pulled up short because he has not thought about the implications of his response in the imposed setting. With training in such drills average students would possibly produce more original responses than in Paulston's communicative drills because of the goad of the teacher's teasing and their natural desire to show him they have recognized his stratagem. This type of drill teeters on the brink of interaction but is still in the area of pseudocommunication and production practice because the whole interchange is teacher-directed with the specific intention of eliciting certain structures.

Where do we go from here? We must work out situations, from an early stage, where the student is on his own, trying to use the language for the normal purposes of language: establishing social relations, seeking and giving information, expressing his reactions, learning to do something, hiding his intentions or talking his way out of trouble, persuading, discouraging, entertaining others, or displaying his achievements. When I say the student is "on his own," I mean he is not supported or directed by the teacher: he may well be working with another or other students. In this type of practice the student should be allowed to use anything he knows of the language and any aids (gestures, drawings, pantomime) to fill out his meaning, when he is "at a loss for words."[12] In this way he will learn to draw on everything he knows at a particular moment in his acquisition of the language, and to fight to put his meaning over, as he would if he suddenly found himself on his own surrounded by monolingual speakers of the language. *This experience is not intended to replace the careful teaching of the language we already supply (the skill-getting activities we organize) but to expand it with regular and frequent opportunities for autonomous interaction, thus making full provision for a dimension of language learning which at present is, if not completely neglected, at least given insufficient place in our programs.* As I have said elsewhere: "Perfection at the pattern-drill level, no matter how impressive to the observer, cannot be an end in itself. It is a fruitless activity unless care is taken to see that the skill gained by such training is further extended until the student is capable of autonomous expression."[13] In 1964, I spoke of the need for developing "that adventurous spirit which will enable [the student] to try to meet any situation by putting what he knows to maximum use."[14] In 1968, I wrote "students should be encouraged, at the advanced level, to try out new combinations of elements to create novel utterances. This is what the advanced student would do were he to find himself in a foreign country. He would make every effort to express his meaning by all kinds of recombinations of the language elements at his disposal. *The more daring he is in such linguistic innovation, the more rapidly he progresses.*"[15] On looking back I feel it was a mistake to tag this recommendation specifically to "the advanced student" (a vague entity at best). Where we have been failing may well be in not encouraging this "adventurous spirit" from an early stage with the result that the student finds it difficult to move from structured security to the insecurity of reliance on his own resources, just as the young would-be swimmer clings to his mother's hand or "the foot on the bottom of the pool."

In Savignon's very interesting study "students in the communicative skills program" (which consisted of one hour per week supplementing the regular audio-lingual type course) "were given the opportunity to speak French in a variety of communicative settings ranging from short (1-2 minute) exchanges between a student and a fluent speaker of French in a simulated situation to whole group discussions on topics of current interest. Emphasis was put on getting meaning across; students were urged to use every means at their disposal to understand and in turn to make themselves understood. Grammar and pronunciation errors were expected and were always ignored when they did not interfere with meaning. In other words, the experimenter and the other fluent speaker who participated in these sessions reacted to what was said, not to how it was said."[16] One student commented: "These sessions taught me to say what I wanted to say instead of book conversations."[17] If we compare this remark with that of the student quoted at the beginning of this paper it seems these students did begin to "talk off the tops of their heads."

Just how practice in autonomous interaction can be incorporated into the program will depend on the type of program, but incorporate it we must, giving it a substantial role in the students' learning. We must not feel that interaction practice is somehow "wasting time" when there is "so much to learn." Unless this "adventurous spirit" is given time to establish itself as a constant attitude most of what is learned will be stored unused, and we will produce learned individuals who are inhibited and fearful in situations requiring language use. With careful selection of the activity, such practice can be a part of every lesson, early in the learning process, with expansion of the complexity of the task as the student advances.

Practice in autonomous interaction should be individualized in the sense that it should allow for the different ways students learn, the different paces at which they learn, the different things which interest them, and the different situations in which they prefer to learn. Students should be offered a choice of tasks (things to do, things to find out, problems to solve, situations to which to react) and then be allowed to choose their own way, their own place, time, and company, for handling them. Some may prefer to work regularly with one other person, others may choose a small group, while other may prefer working with the teacher. Some who are loners will prefer working through certain situations by themselves demonstrating their capacity as individuals (and many of these in a quiet way may outpace their fellows through sheer singlemindedness of purpose).

Students cannot be set down in groups, or sent off in pairs, and told to interact in the foreign language. *Motivation to communicate* must be aroused. Occasionally some fortuitous incident or combination of personalities will cause a desire to communicate something in the foreign language to emerge spontaneously, but mostly it will need to be fostered by the intrinsic interest of the task proposed for the students concerned. Such interest will make the interaction which follows autonomous; a genuine communication from one person to another, not just another imposed act of pseudocommunication. Because of the personal nature of the activity we are promoting, the type of reaction to be displayed must always remain consistent with the personality of the particular student. Some people are temperamentally incapable of interacting with a babble of words; to force them to do so is to force them back into pseudo-communication and into mouthing learned phrases. The quality of the interaction will be judged by other criteria: ability to receive and express meaning, to understand and convey intentions, to perform acceptably in situations and in relations with others.

Earlier I suggested various natural uses of language in interaction which can be used for this type of activity. Here I will expand on these and set down a few elaborations of each; any imaginative teacher will think of many others.

(1) *Establishing and maintaining social relations*: greetings between persons of the same and different age and status, introductions, wishes for special occasions, polite enquiries (with attention to the permissible and the expected questions in the culture), making arrangements, giving directions to strangers, apologies, excuses, refusals, mild rebukes, hedging (the gentle art of noncommunication), encouraging, discouraging, and persuading others. Students might be sent to find out from a monolingual native speaker (or one who pretends to be monolingual) how these are enacted in the cultural context of the language being learned.

(2) *Seeking information* on subjects for which students have some basic vocabulary. (At some point finding out specific technical vocabulary can be part of this type of interaction). Once again the native speaker or informant acts as though he were monolingual, or alternatively the students seek the information from other speakers of the language outside of the course or the school. The information may be useful for (1), for (3), for (4), for (8), or even for (11).

(3) *Giving information* about oneself, one's background, one's country, or about some subject in which one is proficient. The student may be giving information to other students learning to do or make something (4), or passing on information gained in (2). Simulated settings like bank or airline counters, customs desks, workshops, or restaurants may be used where the students are confined to the school setting.

(4) *Learning to do or make something*. Possibilities here are limitless. The pressure of intensive courses can be relieved by organizing actual sessions in the foreign language where students work with real-life materials and activities (sports, hobbies, crafts, physical exercise).

(5) *Expressing one's reactions*. The student can be put in real situations or simulated situations where he has to react

verbally throughout a television show, at an exhibition of pictures or photographs, or during a friendly sharing of slides.

(6) *Hiding one's intentions*. Each student may be given a mission which he must not reveal under any provocation, but which he tries to carry out within a given period of time. This type of activity carries purposeful use of the language beyond course hours as students try to discover each other's missions.

(7) *Talking one's way out of trouble*. Simulated or real situations should be set up of increasing verbal difficulty where the student must use his wits to extract himself from his dilemma.

(8) *Problem solving*. A problem may involve (2) or (4), or even (6) and (7). The problem presented should be an active one whose solution requires verbal activity or enquiry. As early as 1953 Carroll posed the question whether aural-oral methods might not be more successful "if, instead of presenting the student with a fixed, predetermined lesson to be learned, the teacher created a 'problem-solving' situation in which the student must find ... appropriate verbal responses for solving the problem" thus being early forced "to learn, by a kind of trial-and-error process, to *communicate* rather than merely to utter the speech patterns in the lesson plans."[18]

(9) *Sharing leisure activities*. Students should have the opportunity to learn and become proficient in the games and diversions of the foreign culture. They should be able to participate in verbal competitions. Where there are special activities associated with festivals or national holidays these should be engaged in.

(10) *Conversing over the telephone*. This is always difficult in a foreign language and should be practiced early. The student should use a phone book in the foreign language and where this is possible make actual calls enquiring about goods, services, or timetables for transport. The help of monolingual contacts outside the course should be enlisted. (Some incapacitated persons and older people living alone would enjoy participating in this type of activity.) This activity can be linked with (2) or (8), and will often involve (3).

(11) *Entertaining*. The student should be given the opportunity to use his natural talents or encouraged through role-playing sessions to act out in front of a group. He may conduct a radio call-in program or a TV talk show, or groups of students may prepare and present radio or TV commercials (these may involve more or less talking interspersed with mime and are therefore very suitable for the early stages of a course).

(12) *Displaying one's achievements*. Students may tell the group about what they did in (4), (5), (6), (7), or (8), or present and explain special projects. This can be a regular culminating activity to draw together more individualized efforts at interaction.

All of these activities will obviously not be possible for all students from the earliest stage of learning. The teacher will select and graduate activities from these categories so that the attitude of seeking to communicate is developed early in an activity which is within the student's growing capacity. An impossible task which bewilders and discourages the student too early in his language learning is just as inhibiting of ultimate fluency as lack of opportunity to try what he can do with what he knows.

Some people will have deep-seated doubts about accepting such an approach because they foresee that the student will make many errors which may well become ingrained and ineradicable. It was because of such problems that many turned away from the direct method, seeking something more systematic which would seem to ensure more accurate production. Unfortunately, the emphasis on correct production at all times and the firm determination to create a learning situation where students would not make mistakes seems to have led to an impasse for many students. If we wish to facilitate the "great leap" I have described, then a change of attitude toward mistakes during interaction practice is imperative. It is during production (or pseudocommunication) practice that immediate corrections should be made. It is then that we should make the student conscious of possible errors and so familiarize him with acceptable sequences that he is able to monitor his own production and work toward its improvement in spontaneous interaction. In interaction practice we are trying to develop an attitude of innovation and experimentation with the new language. Nothing is more dampening of enthusiasm and effort than constant correction when the student is trying to express his own ideas within the limitations of his newly-acquired knowledge of the language. What is required is for the instructor to note silently consistent and systematic errors made by the student in his presence (not slips of the tongue and occasional lapses in areas where the student usually acquits himself well); these errors will then be discussed with the student at a time when the instructor is helping him evaluate his success in interaction, with particular attention being paid to those types of errors which hinder communication. Such an analytic session may be conducted from time to time with a tape of an actual communication sequence, the student or group of students being asked to detect errors in their own spontaneous production and suggest corrections and improvements. This technique makes the students more alert to their own mistakes and to other possibilities for expressing their meaning which they have not been exploiting.

Many of the types of activities listed may have already found their place in our courses. The originality of the approach lies not so much in the novelty of the activities as in the way in which they are approached. To develop autonomous control of language for communication we must at some time allow the student autonomy, and conversely discourage him from maintaining dependence. We must give the student practice in relying on his own resources and using his ingenuity so that very early in his language learning he realizes that only by interacting freely and independently with others can he learn the control and ready retrieval essential for fluent language use.

FOOTNOTES

[1] *The Advisor* (Teacher-Course Evaluation, University of Illinois, 1970-71), p. 122.

[2]F. Agard and H. Dunkel, *An Investigation of Second-Language Teaching* (Boston: Ginn, 1948), p. 288.

[3]Throughout this paper I have used the terms "foreign language" and "foreign culture" rather than "English" and "American culture" to remind us that for our students English is indeed a foreign language and the American culture a foreign culture.

[4]L. Kelly, *Twenty-five Centuries of Language Teaching* (Rowley, Mass.: Newbury House, 1969).

[5]I have borrowed the division into skill-getting and skill-using from Don H. Parker, "When Should I Individualize Instruction? in *Individualization of Instruction: A Teaching Strategy*, ed. Virgil M. Howes (New York: Macmillan, 1970), p. 176. More detailed explanation of this model can be found in the Report of the Stanford Conference on the Individualization of Foreign Language Instruction (United States Office of Education, 1971), Position Paper on "Techniques for Developing Proficiency in the Spoken Language in an Individualized Foreign Language Program," prepared by Wilga M. Rivers.

[6]"Some Theoretical Aspects of Language Learning and Language Teaching," *Language Learning*, 17(1967), 175.

[7]Michel Benamou and Eugene Ionesco, *Mise en Train* (New York: Macmillan, 1969), "Le professeur est dans la poche du gilet de la montre," p. 44; "Le crocodile est plus beau que Marie-Jeanne," p. 114; "Il dit que ses parents sont aussi grands que la Tour Eiffel," p. 141.

[8]See Chapter 4 of this book, "From Skill Acquisition to Language Control."

[9]*Teaching Foreign-Language Skills* (Chicago: University of Chicago Press, 1968), p. 109.

[10]"Structural Pattern Drills: A Classification," *Foreign Language Annals*, 4(1970), 187-193.

[11]"Teaching Communication," *Language Learning*, 20(1970), 55-68.

[12]S. Savignon used this technique in her "Study of the Effect of Training in Communicative Skills as Part of a Beginning College French Course on Student Attitude and Achievement in Linguistic and Communicative Competence," Ph.D. diss:, University of Illinois at Urbana-Champaign, 1971, since published as *Communicative Competence: an Experiment in Foreign-Language Teaching* (Center for Curriculum Development, 1972).

[13]*Teaching Foreign-Language Skills*, p. 109.

[14]*The Psychologist and the Foreign-Language Teacher* (Chicago: University of Chicago Press, 1964,) p. 78.

[15]*Teaching Foreign-Language Skills*, p. 201. (Italics not in the original.)

[16]Savignon, (1972), p. 25. On pp. 28-9 are listed a variety of communicative tasks used during the practice sessions. Savignon acknowledges her indebtedness to L. Jakobovits, *Foreign Language Learning* (Rowley, Mass.: Newbury House,

1970), Chapter 3, for guidelines in defining these tasks. Professor Jakobovits was the director of her study.

[17]Savignon (1972), p. 30.

[18]J. B. Carroll, *The Study of Language* (Cambridge: Harvard University Press, 1953), p. 188.

3

Contrastive Linguistics in Textbook
and Classroom*

Abstract. The need for a contrastive approach in foreign-language teaching has long been recognized, but in the construction of textbook materials and in classroom practice it has rarely been realized. For pedagogical purposes a useful distinction can be drawn between difference and contrast. Differences can be taught as new items of knowledge, whereas native-language interference must be combatted in areas of contrast. Contrasts should be taught emically not etically, that is, the structural element or the cultural manifestation should be studied as it functions in the foreign language system, not merely at the points where it contrasts with native-language usage. Degree of difficulty may be estimated by the number of elements in contrast, but this criterion does not necessarily apply in the classroom where learning is facilitated if structures can be practiced in an active situation by students who have been prepared for the contrastive nature of language study. Translation may appear to be an excellent exercise in language contrast; it is, however, valuable only at an advanced level of study when students have a wide enough knowledge of the functioning system of both languages to find close-meaning equivalents for stretches of discourse rather than small segments, and to explore the full range of contrast.

*This article reprinted from Monograph No. 21, James E. Alatis, ed., *Contrastive Linguistics and its Pedagogical Implications*, Report of the Nineteenth Round Table Meeting on Languages and Linguistics (Washington, D. C.:Georgetown University Press, 1968), pp. 151-158.

In the past, the empirical judgment of experienced teachers has usually determined the order of presentation and degree of emphasis in textbook materials. Where this judgment has been derived from some systematic observation of student errors it has provided an approximate identification of many areas of language contrast, as evidenced by native-language interference. Gradually the profession has accepted the idea expressed by Fries that 'the most efficient materials are those that are based upon a scientific description of the language to be learned, carefully compared with a parallel description of the native language of the learner'.[1] Yet for some of the languages most commonly taught in our schools and universities, textbooks continue to appear which make little use of the comparative studies which are available while only a small proportion of classroom teachers have the linguistic training to make use of this material without the help of the textbook constructor.

A contrastive analysis of two languages when it is designed with a scientific not a pedagogical intent is not in itself a teaching aid. It must be as exhaustive as its author can make it, in the light of his specific intention, describing with equal care structural contrasts of frequent and of less frequent use or analyzing a limited area in considerable detail. Since the linguist's aim must be to make the description scientifically elegant rather than pedagogically applicable, the analysis will not normally be directly transferable to teaching materials and situations. Chomsky has already emphasized the difference between a linguistic grammar which is an account of competence and a pedagogic grammar which attempts to provide the student with the ability to understand and produce sentences of a particular language.[2] The same distinction may be applied to types of contrastive studies. Fortunately some studies prepared with students' problems in mind are available in the Contrastive Structure Series (University of Chicago Press), although as yet only in a very limited number of pairs of languages.

As Stockwell, Bowen, and Martin have ably demonstrated[3] for pedagogical application a hierarchy of difficulty must be established among the many correspondences. A hierarchy of this type will differ from one established in accordance with purely theoretical premises because 'it is important to distinguish between what may be difficult to explain . . . and what is difficult for the student to internalize—the two may, or may not, be the same'.[4] Once such a hierarchy has been established it must be regarded as 'a set of predictions which must be tested against observation of the problems students do in fact have'.[5] In this article I shall not attempt to duplicate work which has already been done in this area, but shall try to establish certain guidelines for the application of the contrastive approach to classroom work, either by the teacher or textbook constructor.

In the minds of many teachers the notion of contrast is a vague one. It is useful first to distinguish between contrast and difference because each poses a specific pedagogical problem. One language may have a highly developed tone system while another does not. This tone system constitutes a difference of considerable importance, rather than a phonemic contrast. One language may combine elements of various functions in pre-, post-, and medial positions in one unit, whereas the other language may be analytic, arranging elements in linear fashion. In these cases the systems differ to such an extent that comparison of specific elements does not give sufficient information to be pedagogically helpful. For such aspects the new system will need to be taught as an integrated whole without reference to the details of an alien system. For a contrast to be distinguishable at any level, there must be some correspondence at a higher level of structure. Phonemes may contrast in lexical items which are similar in the two languages; there may be contrasting morphemic patterns within syntactic structures of similar applicability (e.g., Language A may require a variety of endings for persons of the verb, as opposed to a simple singular-plural distinction in Language B); within noun phrases there may be a contrasting word order (Language A requiring the order adjective + noun and Language B noun + adjective). If the correspondence is at the level of meaning only, there will be difference rather than contrast: the student will then learn the different way of expressing himself by memorization and practice in appropriate contexts, without reference to the formal characteristics of his native language, and ability to use the new form freely will be a matter of speed of recall. Where there is contrast, native-language interference will be a constant problem: the student's native-language habits will tempt him to follow the pattern of his own language at that point (e.g., using the foreign-language adjective and noun in his native-language pattern of noun + adjective), and intensive practice alone will not be sufficient to free him from this tendency when he is trying to express himself in communication. He will need to be alerted to the specific point at which interference will repeatedly occur, so that he may practice with awareness and concentration and monitor his own production with watchfulness until he finds himself producing the target language forms with ease and accuracy.

Structures will contrast to varying degrees—degree of difficulty for the student being determined theoretically by the number of elements in contrast. In actual language use, however, degree of difficulty will be much more a question of types of choices to be made. Stockwell, Bowen, and Martin[6] have analyzed the possible dilemmas of the student in passing from one language to another in terms of optional choices which the student may make freely in his own or the target language in shaping the meaning he wishes to express, obligatory choices which are the inevitable consequence of his options, and zero choices where the student's problems arise from difference rather than contrast (categories or rules existing in one language but not in the other). In a comprehensive contrastive study emphasis may well fall without distinction on details of the system where there will be greater or less native-language interference or alternatively positive transfer because of structural or functional/semantic correspondence between the native and target languages. When a number of these details operate within a sub-system of the language, where some elements contrast and some are similar in operation, there will be not only the danger of native-language interference at some points but also hesitation and confusion as to the limits of acceptable extrapolation from the native language. At this point, the student must be trained in both that which is similar and that which is contrasting within the sub-system. Many teachers fail at this point and concentrate on teaching only the details which contrast. As a result structures and sub-systems may be taught 'etically' rather than 'emically'. Pike states that 'descriptions or analyses from the etic standpoint are "alien" in view, with criteria external to the system. Emic descriptions provide an internal view, with criteria chosen from within the system. They represent to us the view of one familiar with the system and who knows how to function within it himself.'[7] As soon as a foreign-language structure is taught as though some elements within it function as in the native-language system and some function contrastively, it is not being viewed as a part of the total functioning system of the foreign language, and the student begins to learn the language piecemeal. A student taught in this fashion has great difficulty learning to move freely within the new language system.

The etic approach is frequently employed in teaching the phonological system of a foreign language. Teachers often concentrate on sounds with distinctive features which contrast most obviously with those of otherwise comparable sounds in the native language (i.e., the so-called 'difficult' sounds) while allowing students to produce with native-language articulation sounds with fewer contrasting features. The result is a disruption of the phonological system of the foreign language: sounds produced with incorrect articulatory positions deform neighboring sounds and a 'foreign accent' develops. In concentrating on the sounds which the students find hard to articulate, the teacher often trains them to produce these in such a distinctive and restricted way that the speaker sounds ridiculously pedantic or pretentious to a native speaker, who has learned to produce this sound with variations (within a band of tolerance) dependent on phonological environment or level of discourse. In an emic approach, the student will acquire the phonological system as a functioning whole, learning to discriminate and produce sounds which signal distinctions of meaning within the new language, without being constantly reminded of ways in which it is similar to or different from the phonological system of the native language.

The etic approach may also prevail in the teaching of the grammar of the foreign language. The teacher may concentrate the attention of the students on some feature which functions in a similar fashion in the foreign and native languages at certain points, without making clear the fact that this particular usage is only a restricted part of a wider function which diverges considerably in the two languages. The student may be taught, for instance, that the *futur* in French fulfills the same function as the future tense in English (in *le cortège passera devant l'Hôtel de Ville, passera* fulfills a similar function to *will pass* in *the procession will pass in front of the Town Hall*). This etic type of teaching separates out the forms ... *era*, ... *ira*, ... *ra* from the expression of futurity in the French system of time, and fails to prepare the student for *le facteur va passer dans deux minutes* 'the mailman will be here in two minutes', *je viens dans deux minutes* 'I'll be there in two minutes', and *la direction n'est pas responsable des objets perdus* 'the management will not be responsible for lost property'. The student must learn that what may appear etically to be very different may function emically as one system. What appears to be similar in formation to a structure in the native language may also serve quite a different function in the foreign language, as will soon be clear to a student who, misled by the apparently parallel formation of *I have eaten* and *j'ai mangé,* tries to identify the English present perfect tense with the French *passé composé.*

A similar distinction applies in the teaching of cultural patterns: of values, attitudes, relationships, taboos, and the external manifestations of these. Since language is an integral part of culture, full communication is possible only when the speaker understands the reactions he is arousing in his listener, and the listener is able to identify the intentions of the speaker. In an etic approach, attention is concentrated in the classroom on aspects of external behavior and physically identifiable institutions which appear picturesque and even quaint because they are presented out of the context of interrelationships and functions in the cultural system. As with structural contrasts, that which appears similar may fulfill a contrasting function in the foreign culture while that which appears to contrast by external criteria may have a similar purpose when viewed from within the system. In an emic approach, the teaching of cultural understanding is fully integrated with the process of assimilation of language patterns and lexicon. Through language use, students become conscious of levels of discourse in relation to social expectations, formulas of politeness and what they reveal of social attitudes, and appropriateness of response in specific situations in the foreign culture; through listening and reading they begin to recognize the values which are implicit in much of the foreign behavior. Consequently, instead of being unduly impressed by what is different in the external manifestations of the culture, they come to comprehend contrasts between systems and sub-systems.

From the pedagogical point of view, degree of difficulty must be estimated according to a different set of criteria from those used in a theoretical analysis. A structure which theoretically may be considered more difficult for the student to learn may prove to be less difficult in actual fact because it can be readily transposed into active situations in which the student can practice it frequently. The subjunctive in *il faut que je parte* has usually been relegated by textbook writers to an advanced level in the study of French, yet many students have learned it with ease in the first weeks of study because they have found it useful in communication. Many other structural patterns of wide applicability may be learned similarly at a very early stage despite a high degree of contrast with native-language usage. Stockwell, Bowen, and Martin suggest a criterion of 'functional load' for consideration in establishing a pedagogical sequence of presentation, giving a certain priority to 'patterns which carry a proportionately larger share of the burden of communication'.[8]

From the first lessons students should be prepared by their teacher for the contrastive nature of language formation and function. With this orientation well established, they will be able to absorb many contrasting features of the new language inductively, by a direct method approach, without feeling the need to pause to analyze and describe the differences. A student with such an orientation will more rapidly develop a coordinate language system than a student who is continually seeking to identify in the foreign language equivalents for features in his native language. Mere induction will not suffice, however; to consolidate the use of such contrasting forms, the student will also need systematic drill to develop facility in rapid association of language sequences.

It may appear that the contrastive technique *par excellence* in foreign-language teaching is the translation exercise. Here the student is confronted with native-language forms and structure and required to produce the contrasting forms and structure of the foreign language. It is true that translation in which the exact meaning is transferred from one language to another demands, much more than does speech or original writing, a thorough knowledge of areas of contrast in form and function. It is for this very reason, however, that it is unsuitable as a technique for teaching the details of the language, while being a very profitable and challenging exercise of the student's control of the foreign language at an advanced level. Translation is feasible for the student only when he has a wide enough knowledge of the functioning system of both languages to find close-meaning equivalents for stretches of connected discourse, often longer than one sentence. At the lower levels of instruction students are forced to divide the text into small segments for which they think they can find equivalent segments in the foreign language. Because of the limitations of their knowledge this very segmentation may be an initial source of error as they fail to see the full extent of the contrast in structure.

In the early stages of learning a foreign language, translation of short patterns and simple forms may be a quick way to check whether students have ascribed the appropriate meaning to what they are learning, and whether they have assimilated forms and patterns they have been practicing. In this case the segmentation for purposes of contrast has already been performed for them by the teacher. At an advanced level when students are being taught to translate as a linguistic skill, they should be required to analyze both the source text and their tentative translation for real equivalence. seeking the full extent of the contrasts involved in relation to the context beyond the phrase and the sentence. For such an exercise to provide effective practice in the handling of structural contrast, students should be encouraged to seek a number of alternative solutions in order to explore the full range of contrast, the set of paraphrases they propose in the target language being, to various degrees, meaning-equivalents of the source language sentence or sentences. They should then discuss with each other and with their teacher the contribution of each proposed solution to the elucidation of the basic meaning. They should also be trained to see that effective translation will often involve considerable rearrangement of segments if the full structural possibilities of the foreign language are to be utilized, so that contrasts in forms of discourse will be involved as well as contrasts in structural patterns. When translation is taught at this level of refinement it provides the student with the opportunity to use to the full the knowledge he has accumulated over years of study, and to find by trial and error the acceptable limits of similarity and contrast.

FOOTNOTES

[1] C. C. Fries, *Teaching and Learning English as a Foreign Language* (Ann Arbor: University of Michigan Press, 1945), p. 9.

[2] Noam Chomsky, *Topics in the Theory of Generative Grammar* (The Hague: Mouton, 1966), p. 10.

[3] Robert P. Stockwell, J. Donald Bowen, and John W. Martin, *The Grammatical Structures of English and Spanish*, Contrastive Structure Series (Chicago: University of Chicago Press, 1965); Robert P. Stockwell and J. Donald Bowen, *The Sounds of English and Spanish*, Contrastive Structure Series (Chicago: University of Chicago Press, 1965).

[4] Stockwell, Bowen, and Martin, p. 282.

[5] Ibid.

[6] Ibid., Chapter 11; Stockwell and Bowen, Chapter 2.

[7] K. L. Pike, *Language in Relation to a Unified Theory of the Structure of Human Behavior*, 2nd rev. ed (The Hague: Mouton, 1967), p. 388.

[8] Stockwell, Bowen, and Martin, p. 292.

4

From Skill Acquisition to Language Control[*]

Some years ago, in an attempt to be helpful, I undertook to give some lessons in English to a young Italian immigrant to Australia who happened to have wandered into my church and who was making rather futile efforts to make himself understood with the few words he had acquired haphazardly. Very soon, however, he stopped coming for lessons since it was obvious to him that I did not know how to teach a language. I was trying to make him say things like "I went to work yesterday; I'll go to work tomorrow." This, he was sure, was not the way to learn English. What he wanted to know, and as quickly as possible, was the names of all the things he could see around him.

My young immigrant's attitude reflects a very common misconception about language use: that it is essentially a naming process, that the first step in language acquisition must be the learning of labels for all the features of the environment so as to be able to talk about them to others. Many parents have this idea of language and spend time trying to teach their infants the names of all kinds of objects. Recent studies of child language acquisition, however, show that from their earliest efforts at speech children use words not as mere labels but with the operant force of more fully developed utterances.[1]

---

[*]Originally published in the *TESOL Quarterly* 3 (1969), 3-12.

When a child says "milk," he can mean a number of things. He may be naming a certain familiar liquid; since this desired reaction is rewarded by the obvious pleasure of his parents, he tends to repeat this label to retain their attention. He may repeat the word over and over, engaging merely in word play, enjoying the repetition of sounds and the approving attention he receives as he continues. On the other hand, he may say "milk?" with a look of puzzlement, meaning "Where is my milk? Isn't it time I was fed?" and if he is further ignored he may utter a peremptory "milk!" as a command to his mother to attend to his needs. "Milk. . . ." in a tone of anxiety may mean "Look! I've knocked over my milk. What will happen now?" or it may be a solemn inquiry: "What about my dolly? Isn't she to get a drink too?"

For the child, then, a single word may have all the force of a sentence and carry a number of different meanings, going far beyond its apparent lexical content. Very soon the child expands his utterances to two words, and we see the development of an elementary syntax as he begins to use what Braine has called "pivot" and "open class" words:[2] pivot words forming a small class with few members, frequently repeated, which operate on the larger number of open class words that gradually accumulate as the child's experience broadens. A simple operant like "all gone" ("allgone egg," "allgone milk," "allgone 'nanas") enables the child to extend a basic notion to a number of specific situations. From this stage on, the child's language evolves through a series of syntaxes, identifiable and analyzable at any particular stage of his development; the restricted syntaxes of his early efforts gradually approximate more and more closely to the speech system of those around him until he is finally able to control all its essential syntactic operations. At this stage there is no limit to the number and variety of messages he can convey to fellow speakers of his language. From his earliest attempts at communication, the child needs a grammar; mere labeling will not suffice.

In our second-language classrooms, in recent years we have gone beyond isolated words, mere "vocabulary teaching": we have realized that what the student must learn is to use syntactic patterns. He can acquire new labels later as he requires them, so we teach him a basic vocabulary which he can use over and over again as he practices syntactic operations. We have observed that in the linear sequence of language there are certain strictly formal relationships, within the clearly defined limits of closed sets (e.g., verb systems such as *I'm going, he's going, they're going*). These, we have found, can be learned by steady practice so that no student will be tempted to say* *I's going* or *they's going*. We have found, similarly, that by consistent practice we can teach the restricted word order our language normally requires to convey certain meanings: *I saw him*, not *I him saw* or *Him saw I*. So we have talked of second-language learning as the learning of a skill, the acquiring of a set of habits which must be learned to a point of automatic performance of the sequence. When we are speaking, we do not have time to stop to think about word order, morphological inflections, or invariant syntactical combinations. We need to be so familiar with these details that they fall into place as we speak without distracting our attention from the combinations of meanings we are seeking to express.

This skill-learning approach developed from the common observation that in many classrooms, despite earnest teaching and many exercises on the part of the students, such essential language habits were not being firmly established. Teachers turning to psychological learning theory to see what could be gleaned from it about the effective building in of habits found inspiration in habit formation by reinforcement, or operant conditioning, theory. This approach to learning is drawn from the extensive experimentation of B. F. Skinner and the many experimentalists who have accepted his basic concepts. It has been applied widely in the teaching of many school subjects and is basic to the programming movement.[3]

As applied to teaching techniques and the writing of materials for second-language teaching, Skinner's principles have been interpreted in the following ways.[4] According to Skinner, a response must occur before it can be rewarded, and thus be reinforced. He does not interest himself in what causes the response to occur in the first place. This approach has its obvious application in second-language teaching: naive students cannot invent second-language responses, but these can be elicited by a process of imitation. Imitation is clearly an essential first step in establishing a repertoire of responses in the new language and so we have developed the familiar techniques of mimicking and memorization in elementary second-language classes, as in the memorization of dialogue material repeated after the teacher or tape model. At this stage skill in variation is not sought, but only accurate reproduction.

In conditioning theory, immediate reinforcement or reward increases the probability of a response recurring: the teacher in the second-language classroom supplies this reinforcement by his confirmation of correct responses, as in a pattern drill sequence where the student hears the correct response modeled for him at each step by the teacher or the tape model. With repeated reinforcement, according to the theory, responses become established as habits which are maintained in strength by further reinforcement at intervals as the student uses them to express his meaning in communication. By judicious giving and witholding of reinforcement, responses can be shaped to approximate more and more closely to a desired model. Second-language teachers are familiar with this process which they have long employed for developing finer and finer discriminations in recognition and production of sounds.

Reinforcement after a few occurrences of a response will not, however, ensure that the response will be retained by the student as a permanent feature of his behavior. Unless there is further reinforcement on subsequent appearances, the response-habit will suffer extinction, albeit with some periods of spontaneous recovery before it disappears. For this reason it is essential to reintroduce language material at regular intervals so that the student has the reinforcing, and therefore consolidating, experience of using it correctly on a number of occasions, particularly at the stage when many features of the language are being encountered as novelties in rapid succession. At advanced stages when a great number of features have been integrated into a response framework, the student is forced to draw continually on his previous learning; and his habitual responses, both acceptable and unacceptable, are thus maintained. It is important to remember that incorrect responses will also be reinforced as habitual responses, if the student is not aware of these errors and is satisfied with, and even proud of, his production.

As a repertoire of responses is acquired, Skinner maintains that further responses develop by a process of generalization in which features of novel situations are identified as similar to those already experienced, and established responses find new areas of application. This psychological process is paralleled in second-language learning by the process of analogy as students are encouraged to extend the range of their responses by applying in nearly similar situations the operations they have learned. Analogy is basic to the series of responses in a substitution drill and in other types of exercises which require variation within a limited framework.

A rather naive faith in generalization is perhaps the weakest feature of Skinnerian conditioning as applied to second-language learning. Effective generalization (or production of new utterances by analogy) requires the recognition at an abstract level of a relationship between a new situation and one already familiar, and the combining of new elements in a way which is consistent with this abstract categorization. In a second language where the student's competence (or internalized knowledge of the rules of the language) is partial, this recognition of similarity is guided in really novel situations by his knowledge of parallel structures in his native language. In English we say "I brought it from New York" and "I hid it from John": misled by surface similarities in the native language, the student of French will generalize from "je l'ai rapporté *de* New-York" to "je l'ai caché *de* Jean," instead of the grammatical "je l'ai caché *à* Jean." Valid analogy from one language to another (such as is being investigated in modern studies of language universals) applies at an abstract level of analysis before transformations have produced the distinctive surface features of a particular language.

Even analogizing from one situation in a second language to another in the same language can be misleading. With conditioning techniques the student will have been drilled in transforming utterances either lexically or syntactically to a point of automatic response. Here again he is guided by surface features. In many cases the analogy may be valid; in others the surface features will hide real divergences in usage and the student will fall into error because his knowledge of the language is insufficient for him to recognize the limits within which he may safely analogize.

Despite these limitations, experience has shown that this type of skill practice, systematically developed, does enable students to produce acceptable syntactic patterns on demand in the carefully circumscribed situation of the classroom or laboratory. Properly instructed, the student who is working with the pattern "he's coming" will, on hearing the cue "we," produce the response "we're coming," and continue to produce correct responses even in more complicated sequences. We seem now to have developed techniques for the skill acquisition part of language learning, at least at a formal level. This does not, however, mean that our students on leaving the classroom can participate freely in conversation in the language, producing these acceptable patterns at will. Teachers may well ask: "Where have we been failing? Why are so many of our students after thorough drilling and apparent conditioning still unable to use the language for their own purposes, when spontaneous situations demand more than learned associations?"

Satisfaction with the learning of responses to cues, and even of rapid substitutions, presupposes that language use is the production of language elements in a linear sequence, one item generating the next in succession according to the habit strength of the association. On hearing "Where are you . . .?" most people will complete the utterance with "going." Recent studies of word associations[5] cast considerable doubt on the validity of this approach to the essential processes of language production. Given a cue like "cow," most subjects will produce the response "calf" or "milk," yet sheer strength of linear associations would surely require "cow is . . . ." "Cow, calf" or "cow, milk" rarely appear in succession: word associations are frequently paradigmatic (producing words from the same grammatical class) rather than syntagmatic (or linear) and are drawn from fields of associative structures.[6] To the cue "good," most people will respond "bad" rather than "boy" which would be a common linear or syntagmatic association. (It may be noted that children tend to produce syntagmatic associations more readily than adults. With adults, adverbs produce syntagmatic associations more frequently than other word classes, but even here paradigmatic associations occur.[7])

Perhaps, then, we cite things found together or words frequently occuring in the same utterances. To the stimulus "sword," many will respond with "letter-opener": articles which are conceptually similar but rarely found together or mentioned in close association in speech. Subjects who respond to the cue "fields" with the word "green" are producing neither a paradigmatic nor a syntagmatic association, "green fields" being the association built in by language habits in English. There is clearly an organization among associations which has little to do with linear sequence. Frequency of linear association as the major emphasis in language learning inhibits rather than facilitates real communication. The child learning his native language hears many items in close association, but he does not reproduce these in an automatic fashion. He selects from among them and then uses these selected elements for his own purposes. The child who says "Allgone milk" did not hear the expression in that form. His mother probably said "The milk is all gone" or even "Milk all gone." The child has, at this stage, formed a concept for which he finds the expression "all gone" useful; he then uses "all gone" for his own purposes in a variety of contexts despite his mother's continued repetition of "milk all gone."

In second-language learning, even in a simple structure drill, it is concept formation we should be seeking to bring about, not merely rote learning of items in a sequence. As Miller, Galanter, and Pribram have expressed it: "To memorize the infinite number of grammatical sentences is to by-pass the problem of grammar completely."[8] "The fundamental puzzle . . . is our combinatorial productivity."[9] Even the attempt to memorize a useful selection of sentences for everyday use ignores the real problem that few sentences apart from certain fixed formulas and clichés can be used in an actual situation exactly as learned in the classroom. Just as in perception an association cannot be made with previous percepts before there is recognition of the pattern,[10] so in speech learned associations (sentences, patterns) cannot be useful until the speaker recognizes his requirements for communication as being of a type for which this learned association is appropriate.

Chomsky has attacked the view that language is a "habit structure." He says, "Ordinary linguistic behavior characteristically involves innovation, formation of new sentences and new patterns in accordance with rules of great abstractness and intricacy."[11] He speaks continually of "the creative aspect of normal language use"[12]—the fact that new utterances are similar to those previously heard or produced "only in that they are determined, in their form and interpretation, by the same system of abstract underlying rules."[13] This phrase "creative aspect of normal language use" has led some teachers to think that what is needed is not structural drill but opportunities for the student to "create" new utterances in a free and spontaneous situation, as was formerly the practice in Direct Method classes where students used only the second language from the beginning and tried to communicate in it at all costs. This, as we know, can result in a glib inaccuracy (Frenglish or Spenglish or whatever you will). This carefree indifference to the syntactic demands of the language is certainly not what Chomsky is referring to. According to Chomsky, the speaker-listener must internalize a system of rules that can generate an infinite number of grammatical sentences, and the innovation and creation of which he speaks refer to the production of novel combinations which result from the application of the rules. In this sense our students can only "create" novel utterances when they have internalized the rules, the system of rules then "generating" (in the mathematical sense of this word) new combinations as they require them.

The current vogue for talking about "rules" frightens some teachers. From past experience they know that overt

learning of abstract grammatical rules has not been conspicu-
ously successful in producing students capable of using a
second language creatively, that is, skilled in speaking (listening, reading, writing) without having to hesitate to consider
what is structurally permissible. Chomsky himself uses the
term "internalize" for the assimilation of language rules
because, as he states quite clearly, the speaker-listener is not
generally aware of these rules, "nor in fact is there any reason
to suppose that the rules can be brought to consciousness."[14] Here, he is referring to the native speaker, but a
second-language learner must also reach the point where he is
responding to a rule-system without being aware at each
moment of the rules to which his utterances are conforming.
It is as well to remind ourselves at this point that Chomsky is
not referring to the common "grammar rules" of traditional
textbooks, but to rules of "great abstractness and intricacy,"
the effect of which we observe while being unable to
formulate them at the conscious level. The deep structure
and the transformational rules of which we read in the
literature of generative grammar provide a theoretical model
which does not claim to represent the psychological processes
of language production.

Miller, Galanter, and Pribram have proposed a model of
language production by which we select a higher-level Plan
(or strategy) which sets in operation lower-level plans (or
tactics, i.e., completely detailed specifications of every
operation). [15] In an act of communication, the speaker has a
certain freedom of selection initially (for the meaning he
wishes to express he selects a certain sentence-type, a time
sequence, and certain relationships and modifications within
the sentence), but once this initial selection has been made
there are choices he is obliged to make at lower levels of
structure because of the rule system of the particular
language he is using (obligatory inflections, word order,
function words, substitutes) all of which devolve directly
from his original selection. [16] It is at the level of strategy, or
meaning to be expressed, that the speaker exercises choice,
that the novel or creative element enters in, this choice
necessitating further choices of a more limited character (the

tactics) which oblige the student to use certain elements in fixed relationships. Creative, innovative language use still takes place within a restricted framework: a finite set of formal arrangements to which the speaker's utterances must conform if he is to be comprehended and thus to communicate effectively.

We cannot, then, underestimate the importance of practice in the manipulation of language elements which occur in fixed relationships in clearly defined closed sets (systems in which there are a few variable elements but to which new members are not added: e.g., the set "this, that, these, those"). The student must be able to make the necessary adjustments to pass from "I'*m* going" to "he'*s* staying home." At this level the second-language speaker has no freedom of choice. On the other hand, he may wish to say "I'*d* rather go, but he'*ll* stay" in which case he is operating at the higher level of selection, but once having selected his time sequence and his personal references he has no further freedom at the low level of surface manifestations of tense and person. Unless the student is well trained at this surface level of operation he will not be able to communicate freely the many novel messages he has in mind.

It is at the manipulative level that pattern drills (substitutions and transformations) are valuable. Very early in this century, Thorndike had already shown that direct practice leads to transfer of learning where identical elements are involved: you practice A and B, and you are able to use A and B. Chomsky maintains that in normal language, use of "repetition of fixed phrases is a rarity."[17] This is a very misleading statement because the word "phrase" is undefined. At the level of the sentence, or even for substantial segments of sentences, this is undoubtedly a faithful observation of language performance. If the "phrase" is further subdivided, however, into coherent word groups such as *I'm going, before he comes, if I don't see him,* or *to school* as opposed to *to the station* it becomes clear that numbers of segments reappear again and again in identical form, and it is segments like these—the building blocks of the utterance—that are practiced in drills.

On the other hand, Katona discovered that for problem solving an understanding of structural principles led to greater facility in solving new problems and also to longer retention. "We do not learn the examples," he said, "we learn *by* examples. The material of learning is not necessarily the object of learning: it may serve as a clue to a general principle or an integrated knowledge." [18] This is the Gestalt concept of transposition: ". . . the elements are changed, but the whole-qualities, the essence, the principle are preserved in recollection. . . . and we may apply them under changed circumstances." [19] It is at the level of selection, of conscious choice, that the second-language speaker must have a clear conception of the possibilities of variation within the structural system, of the principles which determine the sentence framework and the relationships of the parts within it, so that he is able to set in motion the various elements which will combine in the ways he has learned so thoroughly in order to convey the exact meaning he has in mind. It is this aspect of second-language learning which has been largely neglected in recent years.

The student will acquire this realization of the possibilities of application and combination of what he is learning, not by listening to lengthy abstract explanations (tempting as this activity may be for the teacher), but by using the structural patterns he is learning, in combination with what he has learned, for some purpose of his own. It is not sufficient for him to use a pattern to complete an exercise or to answer as the teacher requires; he must practice selection, from the earliest stages of instruction, in an attempt to combine what he knows and what he is learning in the expression of a message he has personally chosen. (It is in this activity that, under the teacher's guidance, he learns the extent of permissible extrapolation or analogy.) No matter how simple the pattern, it is important in the communication system for its possibilities of occurrence and combination, and it takes its place in the second-language system the student is building up as soon as it becomes a medium of communication, rather than a simple manipulative operation.

All this may seem to be far away from the practical demands of the teaching situation. How, the teacher may ask, can I apply this in the classroom? The following suggestions will, I hope, lead my readers to work out their own applications in conformity with the theoretical position I have been discussing.

Dialogue learning is a common classroom activity for which useful techniques have long been outlined. Nevertheless in using dialogue material many teachers never pass beyond the stage of manipulation: the dialogue is thoroughly memorized; groups, rows, individuals make the appropriate exchanges. The teacher now passes to the next part of the unit. In this type of lesson the essential ingredient of role-identification is missing. As soon as the child acts out the dialogue, as soon as he *is* John or Peter, he is communicating, not merely repeating. Even the inhibited child will speak out if he is being someone else. This acting out of dialogues by various children is not a waste of time. Children will repeat the same material over and over purposefully, and listen attentively to others repeating it if different groups are reliving the roles. When children act out a recombination of the dialogue (one learned from the textbook or one they have themselves created using the well-known segments), they explore further possibilities of combination and application of each pattern to express a variety of meanings. In this way they are preparing for the act of selection when later they wish to express similar meanings. Acting out a dialogue makes even memorization a meaningful activity instead of an artificial classroom technique: even great actors must memorize their roles, and memorization is thus accepted as a normal activity of real life.

Pattern drilling, as teachers well know, may become a parrot-like activity. Even with variations, the student familiar with the technique soon learns to make the necessary adjustments without having to concentrate his attention to the point of personal involvement. When, however, the student asks a question or gives an answer related to someone or something which concerns him personally, even an item in a drill becomes a form of communication. Intensive practice need not, and should not, be divorced from real situations. The lexical content of the drills should be applicable to things the student experiences in and out of the classroom, so that the items are useful even apart from the practice; they should provide meanings with which the student can identify. An alert teacher can easily develop a practice sequence which could feasibly apply to the situation of some or all of the students, with an element of humor or surprise to keep the students' interest. Visual cues for drills not only keep the student alert but force him to think for himself, instead of merely adapting what the teacher is voicing for him. In a carefully structured lesson, the students can be stimulated to provide the elements of the drills themselves: they can be provoked into making a series of statements or questions of the pattern desired through what are apparently only comments on the teacher's appearance or activities, or on their own or other students' intentions or interests. Many a pattern drill can be converted into a repetitive but exciting game which demands concentration. In all of these ways, participation in the drill can be innovative: providing for practice in the repetition and variation of language segments, but with simultaneous practice in selection, as the student expresses his own meaning and not that of the textbook writer. A tape-recording of such a lesson may not sound very different from one made during a stereotyped pattern drill session, the responses of the students following a familiar sequence. The difference, however, is not physical, but psychological: the active participation of the students is personal. Practice in selection should not be considered a separate activity for advanced classes: it can and should be included in class work from the very first lessons.

To sum up then, the student cannot perform effectively at the higher level of selection (putting into operation higher-level choices) unless facility has been developed in the effortless production of interdependent lower-level elements. So learning by intensive practice and analogy variation, under the teacher's guidance, will be features of the early stages of learning a second language, but with immediate practice in selection (within the limits of the known). The student will be continually placing new elements in the context of the functioning system as he understands it at that stage, by interrelating the new with the old. For this he will need to understand what he has been trying to do in his practice exercises. He will be kept continually aware of the relationship of what he is learning to what he knows, so that he can fully realize the systematic function of each new element he has practiced through his endeavors to use it in wider contexts for the expression of his own meaning.

To develop skill in communication in the foreign language the student must have continual practice in communicating, not merely in performing well in exercises, no matter how carefully these may have been designed. The teacher's reward comes on the day when he hears his students using the second language without prompting and without embarrassment for communicating their own concerns. This is language control. When the student has acquired confidence at this level, he will be able to progress on his own, experiencing freedom of expression beyond the confines of learned patterns.

FOOTNOTES

[1] D. McNeill, "Developmental Psycholinguistics," *Genesis of Language*, eds. F. Smith and G. A. Miller (Cambridge, Mass.: MIT Press, 1966).

[2] M. Braine, "The Ontogeny of English Phrase Structure: the First Phase," *Language*, 39 (1963): 1-13.

[3] See B. F. Skinner, *The Technology of Teaching* (New York: Appleton-Century-Crofts, 1968).

[4] The appropriateness of Skinnerian conditioning in second-language teaching has been discussed fully in Wilga M. Rivers, *The Psychologist and the Foreign-Language Teacher* (Chicago: University of Chicago Press, 1964).

[5] See J. Deese, *The Structure of Associations in Language and Thought* (Baltimore: Johns Hopkins Press, 1965).

[6] "Cow's milk" does appear, but is a different sequence.

[7] Deese, p. 106, gives a table of frequencies of occurrence. For observations of children's associations, see S. Ervin, "Changes with Age in the Verbal Determinants of Word Association," *American Journal of Psychology*, 74 (1961): 361-72.

[8]G. A. Miller, E. Galanter, and K. Pribram, *Plans and the Structure of Behavior* (New York: Holt, 1960), p. 147.

[9]G. A. Miller, *Psychology and Communication* (New York: Basic Books, 1967), p. 79.

[10]The "Hoffding function." See U. Neisser, *Cognitive Psychology* (New York: Appleton-Century-Crofts, 1967), p. 50.

[11]"Linguistic Theory," *Language Teaching: Broader Contexts,* ed. R. Mead, Jr., Report of Northeast Conference on the Teaching of Foreign Languages (New York: MLA Materials Center, 1966), p. 44.

[12]See also *Topics in the Theory of Generative Grammar* (The Hague: Mouton, 1966), p. 11.

[13]"Linguistic Theory," p. 44.

[14]*Topics*, p. 10.

[15]Miller, Galanter, and Pribram, pp. 16, 139-58.

[16]This approach to language production is discussed at length in Wilga M. Rivers, *Teaching Foreign-Language Skills* (Chicago: University of Chicago Press, 1968), pp. 71-80.

[17]"Linguistic Theory," p. 46.

[18]G. Katona, *Organizing and Memorizing* (New York: Columbia University Press, 1940), p. 125.

[19]Katona, p. 136.

5

Motivating Through Classroom Techniques[*]

How often we hear teachers complaining about their students:

"What can I do? They just *lack motivation*." This, of course, is an impossible statement. Every living organism to survive must have some motivation. Frymier has defined motivation as "*that which* gives direction and intensity to behavior."[1] This type of definition emphasizes the fact that little is known about motivation which, in psychological terms, is a construct inferred from the way an organism behaves. (By the direction and intensity of the behavior we infer something about the inner state of the organism, and in order to be able to discuss and investigate this "something" we call it motivation.)

The complaint: "*They just have no motivation to learn to speak English*" may be a more accurate description of the behavior of some students in school, but even this statement usually reflects a lack of realization on the part of the speaker of the complex and individual nature of motivation. Certain experiments have been performed where teachers had the opportunity to instruct by way of an intercom system

---

[*]A paper read at the TESOL Conference in New Orleans, 1971.

fictitious students and then saw their supposed work. These experiments have shown that the teacher's conviction about the degree of intensity of a student's motivation may reflect the picture the teacher has created for himself of this particular student rather than the student's actual psychological state.[2] The students to whom our teacher is referring in the complaint just voiced may not lack motivation to learn to speak English but may have found what seems to the teacher to be substandard, or even incorrect, English quite sufficient for their communicative purposes in the community in which they live. This may also be the only variety of English they hear from those with whom they wish to identify: parents or neighborhood associates. All indispensable communication, as far as they are concerned, may take place in Spanish or Turkish or Navajo. The real problem for the teacher may be: *"My students have no motivation to learn what I teach in my English class."*

So the question, *"How can I motivate my students?"* is not well formulated, nor is the question: *"How can I motivate my students to learn?"* Our students may not appear to be learning what we are earnestly trying to teach them, but every organism, nevertheless, is continually learning. As John Holt tries to show in *How Children Fail*, our students may be learning in our classrooms to protect themselves from embarrassment, from humiliation, and from other emotional concomitants of failure; they may be learning to give us "the right answer and the right chatter."[3] According to Postman and Weingartner "a classroom is an environment and . . . the way it is organized carries the burden of what people will learn from it":[4] consequently, some of our students may be learning from our classrooms that the use of English is a rather meaningless, mechanical activity, or even that it is a vehicle for a teacher's monologues. In either case it would seem to them clearly unrelated to their own concerns or interests.

There are two main strands of psychological thought on the question of motivation:[5] the hedonistic strand which includes the various theories of reinforcement or reward, and the ego-involvement strand in which the individual's self-image and level of aspiration play the determining role.

The hedonistic approach goes back at least as far as Thorndike's Law of Effect. It is discernible in the explanations of many psychologists and notably in those which emphasize reinforcement or reward, and in the pleasure principle of Freud. According to this approach, the individual organism in its relations with the environment is continually seeking to safeguard a state of equilibrium or balance of tension which it finds pleasurable. Excess of motivation disrupts this balance and causes increase in tension which the organism actively seeks to reduce by purposeful goal-directed behavior. Just as excess of motivation is painful to the organism, so is frustration in its goal-seeking efforts which prevents the organism from regaining its state of equilibrium. In this view, motivation can be looked upon as a continual process of individual adjustment to the environment. The individual actively seeks experiences which are pleasurable and avoids those which are painful. This parsimonious view of motivation would seem to provide a straightforward guideline for the classroom teacher. Unfortunately, because of the complexity of the inner state of each organism what is pleasurable for one is not necessarily pleasurable for another, and the teacher must keep these individual differences in mind.

Basically this view would indicate that the teacher should capitalize on the learner's motivated state by keeping the work within the capacity of each student so that he experiences success which is tension-reducing and rewarding. This is the basis of the programmed learning approach. In a well-designed programmed text attainable goals, clearly discernible in carefully elaborated steps, act as incentives and, as each is completed, the student is given immediate confirmation of the correctness or incorrectness of his response. This continual feedback provides reinforcement of what has been learned so that each student is motivated to continue to reproduce responses which have been rewarded and to put forth effort in the hope of experiencing further reinforcing success. Ideally such a stage can be reached by each student only in a completely individualized program where each person proceeds at his own pace. Unfortunately, completely individualized work as presently developed in programmed texts or computer-assisted instruction appears to conflict with the concept of language as primarily a vehicle of communication in which at least two persons by their interaction influence and modify each other's production. We must wait for further technological development of audio components and more imaginative programming before this disability can be overcome. In any case sophisticated materials of this type are still beyond the financial capacities of most schools. In the average classroom the teacher does the best he can in distributing reinforcement within the class group, or within smaller groups for particular activities, hoping in this way to shape behavior progressively in the direction he desires. The result is a classroom largely teacher-dominated as the teacher seeks to manipulate the environment to provide the most favorable conditions for inducing correct language behavior on the part of as many of the students as possible.

The second distinctive view of motivation which is reflected in much modern writing on educational problems maintains that the individual is continually seeking that which enhances his self as he perceives it, that is, that he is striving to achieve what he perceives as his potential. The student is, then, motivated at first in a general, nonspecific way in any situation—in other words, he is ready to take from any situation what there is in it for him. This initial motivation energizes and directs the student's behavior, causing him to attend to and focus on what is new in his environment. This attention is facilitative of learning but must be caught and maintained. It is at this stage that the teacher uses interest-arousing techniques to involve the student. The student is more readily involved if the teacher builds on areas of concern to him at his particular stage of development, thus making the new learning meaningful and increasing its incentive value. Many psychologists believe that the human organism possesses certain autonomous impulses such as curiosity, the desire to know and to understand, the desire to play and explore, and the impulse to manipulate features of the environment. These provide raw material with which the teacher can work to interest the student in the learning process. Through success in language activities and through the satisfaction of recognized and recognizable achievement the student comes to take an interest in the subject for its own sake (that is, an intrinsic interest in learning to know and use English) and what is sometimes called a cognitive drive which is self-sustaining then develops.[5] The development of such an interest in learning English for its own sake is, of course, the final aim of the teacher of English and the best assurance that the student will continue to learn and to seek opportunities to use English after the classroom has ceased to provide his learning environment.

In this latter view, a student's reaction to a stimulus is not predictable from the external conditions as the teacher sees them, but is determined by the student's individual perception of reality. The student may perceive a particular situation as a threat and withdraw from it or react unpredictably to counteract it. This is likely to happen quite frequently in an authoritarian classroom and many English-teaching classrooms are authoritarian: the teacher knows English well, the student does not, and therefore the teacher is always right and always correcting the student. In such situations many a student is forced to adopt strategies to protect his self-image, even, in some cases, to the extent of preferring to be wrong in the first place because at least in this way he knows where he stands and the outcome is less painful. Another student may set himself unrealistic goals which he cannot possibly attain because certain failure which he can blame on someone else is less damaging for him than unexpected failure where he expected to succeed. The teacher who understands this personal character of motivation can help individual students to set themselves attainable goals, no matter what their degree of aptitude, thus building up their self-confidence and increasing their motivation.

Whichever approach to motivation we accept (and as classroom teachers we can learn something of value from each of them),[6] it is clear that motivation is a normal state of the individual. It is for the teacher to identify its individual character and channel it through his design of learning activities. Of itself, motivation is merely raw material.

In the scope of this paper I can consider only a few of the implications of the theoretical positions described, but in each case I shall show how classroom practice in a particular situation will be affected if what is known about motivation is kept in mind.

First of all, *the student is motivated to learn*. We begin, whether we realize it or not, with a motivated organism in front of us. But what, we must ask ourselves, is this student motivated to learn? Perhaps he is motivated to learn enough English to communicate his needs, but not to slog away at uninteresting exercises.

But aren't these exercises necessary? the teacher may ask. What does "learning English" consist of?

- —learning to pronounce certain sounds in certain environments;
- —learning to use certain lexical items in certain contexts;
- —learning to manipulate certain patterns which we can then incorporate into more extensive patterns to express the fullness of our meaning;
- —learning to recognize sound-symbol relationships;
- —learning to extract meaning from sound or graphic sequences?

As listed, these activities may seem quite irrelevant to Maria or George.

So we narrow down our aims more and more, and we state our behavioral objectives very precisely: we want Maria and George

- —to learn to distinguish /I/ from /i/ and to learn to pronounce /t∫/;
- —to learn to ask an information or a yes-no question;
- —to learn six parts of the body.

Maria or George may still not be motivated to learn what the teacher has prepared. It is fine for the teacher to "state behavioral objectives" but Maria and George will still not learn unless they see these objectives as relevant to their personal goals. Maria may want to be able to buy some *potato chips* without being asked to repeat what she said over and over again. George may want to be able to ask the price of a comic book or to find out how a battery-powered fire engine works. Carmelita may want to be able to say "That's *my* ball."

How do we achieve our behavioral objectives and those of our students? For some teachers an exercise is an exercise is an exercise (or a drill is a drill is a drill). All exercises (or drills) can be personalized. Only if distinguishing /ʃ/ and /t / are seen as communication problems will Maria be interested, and pronunciation problems can be treated in a communication situation. So can parts of the body, but not in the old format where the teacher asks: "Do I have two heads? Do you have three feet?" This is not even a pretence at authentic communication. A game of *Simon Says* where children have to touch or move parts of the body in the rapid sequence of the competition is a communication situation. Listening to something to which one has to react by drawing something or doing something is communication. Reading something to find out information for one's own interest or in order to tell someone else something is communication. A student who says: "Where are you going tonight?" to another student and expects a reply is learning to communicate. If he says exactly the same words in a mechanical fashion as part of a drill or dialogue because the teacher says this is what he should do, he is learning to do an exercise: he is learning to give "the right answer and the right chatter." This psychological difference is crucial. Remember that the student learns from the classroom, from your structuring of the learning activities, whether English is for communication or not. He learns whether it is part of his reality or just some tedious, artificial chore which someone "up there" has ordained he must perform. Exercises, oral or written, should always be framed as communication exercises: with a credible sequence of ideas and with some relevance to the class group and the class situation (which are the child's reality during his school years). If you lack imagination, learn to involve that of your students. Remember that a student whose interests and concerns are considered respectable and worthwhile in the classroom develops an enhanced perception of himself which increases his motivation to involve himself in purposive behavior within the class group.

What about the child's impulses to play, to explore, to manipulate? These can certainly be harnessed to the language teacher's endeavor. Recently I saw a first grade class in an elementary school bilingual project practicing the full paradigm in Spanish of the verb "to go"—I go, you go, he goes, we all go. . . . A few minutes earlier they had all been lying on mats for their rest period. What an opportunity was being missed! Children of this age love to imitate and mimic. They love make-believe and they identify rapidly with roles which they act out with great enthusiasm. They love movement and they can hardly curb their desire to express themselves vocally. They love stories with much repetition and they insist on each story being repeated exactly as before. Repetitive rhymes and songs are their delight. Instead of look-and-listen activities, or even listen-and-repeat activities, they become absorbed in *listen-do-repeat activities* where they concentrate on the active meaning of what they are saying. And they practice spontaneously at home, showing Mommy and Daddy how it is done, and proudly singing their new song to aunts and uncles. What an opportunity was being missed in that classroom by an elementary school teacher who, suddenly asked to teach Spanish, could think only of how she was taught long ago, instead of exploiting her knowledge of the characteristics and interests of the young child. (In this class too, may I add, many of the children spoke Spanish as a mother tongue.)

It is not only very young children who learn through movement. Many students from lower socio-economic levels where the home environment is not verbal and abstract respond to concrete material for which they see an immediate application. They enjoy learning words and phrases which they can employ immediately in the context of the class or with other children—in the neighborhood or in the school ground. They also learn through activity: through seeing, hearing, touching, manipulating, and through role-playing. The teacher should use visual presentations (flash cards, drawings, projected material); things students can hold, open, shut, pass to each other; music, songs with tapes, guitars, drums; action songs, action poems. The vocabulary taught should be practical; the characters and incidents they hear or read about should never appear to be "prissy" or effeminate. By building on the known characteristics of different types of students we are using their existing motivation for our pedagogical purposes.

We must find out what our students are interested in. This is our subject matter. As language teachers we are the most fortunate of teachers—all subjects are ours. Whatever the children want to communicate about, whatever they want to read about, is our subject matter. The "informal classroom" we hear so much of these days[7] is ours if we are willing to experiment. Do our students watch TV? This we can use by incorporating material they are all watching into our class-room programs. The essence of language teaching is providing conditions for language learning—using the motivation which exists to increase our student's knowledge of the new language: we are limited only by our own caution, by our own hesitancy to do whatever our imagination suggests to us to create situations in which students feel involved— individually, in groups, whichever is appropriate for the age level of our students in the situation in which we meet them. We need not be tied to a curriculum created for another situation or another group. We must adapt, innovate, improvise, in order to meet the student where he is and channel his motivation.

As we design our program it should be possible to involve students in the selection of activities according to their personality preferences. Should all students, even the inartic-ulate, be expected to want to develop primarily the speaking skill? Some children reared on television may feel more at ease if allowed to look and listen with minimal oral participation until they feel the urge to contribute: these children will learn far more if allowed to develop according to their own personality patterns than if they are forced to chatter when they have nothing to say. Teachers, too, should be aware of psychological research which shows that native language development proceeds at a different rate for girls and boys,[8] with the girls advancing more rapidly, and that the effect of this difference is cumulative. At certain stages, then, one may expect girls to express themselves orally more readily than boys and this again affects differentially their reaction to chattering in a foreign language. Some students may prefer to range beyond the rest of the class in reading and for such children graded reading material for individual selection, covering a wide variety of topics, should be readily available.

Such individualization of choices requires imaginative planning by the classroom teacher who should be willing and ready to go beyond a uniform diet for all comers as soon as children's individual styles of learning make themselves apparent. An experimental study reported by Politzer and Weiss shows that "better results were obtained by the pupils of those teachers who went beyond the procedures strictly prescribed by the curriculum, teachers who were concerned with supplementing the curriculum rather than merely implementing it." It seems, according to this report, that "the efficiency of the individual teacher increase(d) with the amount of his *personal* stake and *personal* contribution to the instructional processes."[9] Can this be less so for the student himself? We know that involvement in personally selected tasks is intrinsically motivating to normal students. This further source of motivation we must not neglect if we wish to channel the student's natural energies.

Ausubel has pointed out that "motivation is as much an effect as a cause of learning."[10] The relationship between the two, he says, is "typically reciprocal rather than unidirectional."[11] By this he means that when we capitalize on the student's initial motivation, focus it, and direct it into satisfying ego-enhancing learning experiences then this satisfaction motivates the student to further learning along these lines. Nothing breeds success like success. As one meaningful learning task after another is mastered, the attractiveness of the tasks increases and the student is motivated to "practice, rehearse, and perform what he has already learned."[12] What more could we seek as language teachers?

In all of this who is the experimenter? It is not the expert nor the consultant but the classroom teacher—the teacher who one day says to himself: "I think I'll reorganize what I have been doing and see if some of these things I have been hearing really work." Progress in improvement of the conditions for learning comes not through funded projects here and there but through the thousands, the millions of classrooms in operation every hour of the week. There has been much enthusiasm in recent years for educational improvement, but from a study of some two hundred and sixty classrooms Goodlad concluded in 1969 that "most of the so-called educational reform movement has been blunted on the classroom door."[13] What of the bilingual program? What of the English as a second language and second dialect programs throughout the country? Their fate too lies behind the classroom door. In other words, they are your personal responsibility. Think of this next time you go into your classroom.

FOOTNOTES

[1]J. Frymier, "Motivation: The Mainspring and Gyroscope of Learning," *Theory into Practice*, 9(1970): 23.

[2]T. Johnson, R. Feigenbaum, and M. Weiby, "Some Determinants and Consequences of the Teacher's Perception of Causation," unpublished manuscript, University of Wisconsin, 1964, cited by W. B. Waetjen in "The Teacher and Motivation," *Theory into Practice*, 9(1970): 13-14.

[3]New York: Dell, 1970, p. 42. Originally published by Pitman, 1964.

[4]N. Postman and C. Weingartner, *Teaching as a Subversive Activity* (New York: Delacorte, 1969), p. 18.

[5]D. Ausubel, *Educational Psychology: A Cognitive View* (New York: Holt, Rinehart and Winston, 1968), pp. 367-68.

[6]The subject of motivation and implications from theory for classroom practice is dealt with at length in Wilga M. Rivers, *The Psychologist and the Foreign-Language Teacher* (Chicago: University of Chicago Press, 1964), chap. 9.

[7]See, for instance, C. E. Silberman, *Crisis in the Classroom* (New York: Random House, 1970).

[8]Dorothea A. McCarthy, "Sex Differences in Language Development" in *Psychological Studies of Human Development*, eds. R. G. Kuhlen and G. G. Thompson (New York: Appleton-Century Crofts, 1970), pp. 349-53.

[9]R. L. Politzer and L. Weiss, "Characteristics and Behaviors of the Successful Foreign Language Teacher," Stanford Center for Research and Development in Teaching, Technical Report No. 5 (Palo Alto, April 1969) pp. 69-70.

[10]Ausubel, p. 393.

[11]Ausubel, p. 365.

[12]Ausubel, p. 385.

[13]Quoted in Silberman, p. 159.

6

The Foreign-Language Teacher
and Cognitive Psychology
or Where Do We Go from Here? *

Martin Braine, the eminent psycholinguist, tells the story about his two-and-a-half-year-old daughter who had the habit of using "other one" as a noun modifier, as in "other one spoon." On a number of occasions he tried to induce her to utter the correct form "the other spoon." A typical interchange went as follows: "Want other one spoon, Daddy"—"You mean, you want THE OTHER SPOON."— "Yes, I want other one spoon, please, Daddy"—"Can you say 'the other spoon'?"—"Other . . . one . . . spoon" —"Say . . . 'other' " —"Other" —"Spoon" —"Spoon" —"Other . . . spoon" —"Other . . . spoon. Now give me other one spoon?"[1] Braine uses this as an example to show that children have difficulty in using negative information (that is, correction) for the development of their syntax, a feature of child learning that has been observed by many researchers.

Any foreign-language teacher must nod understandingly on hearing a story such as this and think of similar experiences he has had: when, for instance, after careful and apparently successful practice of the form of a question a student raises his hand and asks, "What means this word, Miss X?"[2] And so our problems continue perennially. It does not

---

*Keynote address at the Central States Conference on the Teaching of Foreign Languages, 1972.

surprise us when, in this period of innovations, the student working on his individualized packet on the mysterious workings of the direct object in French looks up as his facilitator of learning[3] comes to his carrel in the learning center and says: "*Je comprends le très bien*." External arrangements may be different, our attitude to our students' learning may have changed so that the pace of activities, even the type of activity, has been adjusted to individual styles, but the problems of language learning remain: those peculiar problems which make the learning of a foreign language a different proposition from the learning of history or science or home economics.

We certainly do not lack statements on how we should go about our task of helping a student to acquire a second language. In fact we seem at times to be almost deafened by a babble of voices. One rather prevalent (and to my mind oversimplified) view is described by Cooper in the following terms: "There seems to be little evidence that the actual language-learning *processes* differ for the child and the adult. Somehow, both have to abstract the linguistic rules underlying the language as well as the sociolinguistic rules underlying its use. Some second-language learners may do this more quickly than others . . . but they must do it nonetheless if they are to learn the language. The question which confronts us as language teachers is how we can best structure the language-learning situation so as to exploit the language-learning abilities of the student."[4] The type of restatement in the last sentence, if taken at its face value, obviously does not throw a great deal of light on the problem. It does, however, highlight the need for us as teachers to know as much as we possibly can about the way the student learns and learns language. The approach in the passage cited is that of a number of writers in recent journals who are trying to reexamine teaching problems in the light of the latest findings of linguistics and psychology.

When we discuss language-learning processes at the level of generality of Cooper's statement we must not be surprised to read that these "processes" do not differ for the child and the adult. It is almost self-evident that the language learner must "abstract" and internalize as a part of his own cognitive structure the system of linguistic and sociolinguistic rules if he is to function autonomously in the language, independently of his teacher. We are not surprised, at this undifferentiated level, when the writer tells us that he must do this "somehow."

Basic to Cooper's statement is a theory expounded in several places by Chomsky[5] that the child has innate language-learning abilities in the form of "a linguistic theory that specifies the form of the grammar of a possible[6] human language" and a "strategy for selecting a grammar of the appropriate form that is compatible with the primary linguistic data,"[7] that is, for matching with the language he hears around him (Chomsky calls it "meagre and degenerate data"[8]) the form of a particular grammar from a "fairly restricted set of potential languages".[9] The "strategy" of which Chomsky is speaking is a language acquisition device (LAD)[10] which proceeds by hypothesis-testing. The child makes hypotheses about the form of the grammar of the language to which he is attending. He compares this with his innate knowledge of the grammar of a possible language[11] which is congruent with the abstract principles of universal grammar and which is capable of generating through ordered sets of transformations the many surface variations of this specific language. (Note that the hypotheses the child is presumed to be making are about deep structure relationships, not the peculiarities of surface structure.)

It is against this theoretical background that we can now consider Cooper's proposals for an actual language teaching situation. Quoting from an article by Vivian Cook,[12] he suggests that the teacher should "permit, and indeed encourage the learner to produce sentences that are ungrammatical from the point of view of the target language. This would be done on the assumption that . . . the second language learner's deviations are not random but systematic and reflect implicit hypotheses as to the nature of the language being learned . . . When he produces sentences which deviate from those of the target language, the teacher's reactions can help him change the hypotheses. Note that the teacher would be more concerned with correcting the *hypothesis* underlying the deviant sentence than with inducing the student to correct the particular *sentence.*"[13] Now I certainly agree that we should give our students abundant opportunity to experiment in spontaneous use of the language, knowing full well that in doing so they will produce some ungrammatical sentences. In Article 2, "Talking off the Tops of Their Heads," I have advocated that such opportunities be provided as early as possible in the student's language-learning experience, in association with the structured teaching sequence. This type of free-wheeling gives the student opportunities to try what he can do with what he knows: making "infinite use of finite means" (to use the oft-quoted phrase of Humboldt). It is during such autonomous interaction that we can see what systematic errors the student is making and correct his erroneous hypotheses about the structure of French, or German, or English.

What I am interested in, then, is not so much what is being proposed here but its theoretical underpinnings. First of all, linguistically speaking, it cannot be considered an application in teaching practice of Chomskyan theory. The child's hypotheses about which Chomsky is speaking are, as we have noted, at the abstract level of deep structure. Since the child's knowledge of the grammars of possible languages is said to be innate, his hypotheses about the nature of the language to which he is attending cannot really be deviant and in need of correction, if our interpretation of the theory is consistent. Chomsky says "various formal and substantive universals are intrinsic properties of the language—acquisition system, these providing a schema that is applied to data and that determines in a highly restricted way the general form and, in part, even the substantive features of the grammar that may emerge upon presentation of appropriate data."[14] It is in this sense that the utterances of children learning their first language are no longer considered "errors" by developmental psychologists who base their interpretations on the innateness theory, but rather exemplars of basic structural relations.[15] Extrapolating directly from linguistic theory to classroom practice is not as simple as the quotation from Cooper would make it appear.

In a laudable enthusiasm to keep language teaching practice congruent with the latest theories in other disciplines there seems to be a recent tendency to brush aside what the older learner brings to the second-language learning experience.[16] In the classroom situation that Cooper is describing, the deviations which are "ungrammatical from the point of view of the target language" are clearly at the surface structure level and do not reflect "implicit hypotheses as to the nature of the language being learned" in the sense in which Chomsky has used these terms. We are clearly talking about a different type of hypothesis. As every experienced teacher knows, one of the principal hypotheses underlying the deviant utterances of an older student learning a second language is that the surface structure of the new language will closely duplicate the surface structure of his first language. The first-language learner who hears only surface realizations of the underlying rules of the particular language he is learning (interspersed with some performance errors) and who is surrounded during all his waking hours by the language he is trying to acquire does not have this conflict in his natural language-learning situation. He detects logical relations and begins in a basic fashion to express these relations. It is these relations, as Lakoff has recently observed,[17] which are a part of universal grammar. This explains why young children learning different languages seem to pass through similar developmental phases, producing similar early grammars which represent the same basic relations before they reach the stage of differentiation of the details of the surface structure of the particular language they are acquiring. When, however, even a young child learns a second language, still in a natural, untutored fashion, we have evidence that he too suffers from the interference of the surface features of one language with the surface features of the other.[18]

When the adult learner discovers that many features of the two surface structures are not comparable in their functioning he frequently overcompensates by overgeneralizing divergent features of the new language to instances where the two systems do in fact coincide. (Having learned that a French adjective frequently follows the noun as in *une pomme rouge*, he will overgeneralize to *un crayon long* where the order paralleling the English order, *un long crayon*, would have been appropriate.) The recent research in error analysis reported by Jack Richards[19] shows over half the errors he cites to be interference errors while among the remaining overgeneralization errors many are overcompensatory. Learning the limits of generalization of specific rules in a new language is a problem which can often be handled better by direct instruction, which highlights differences in the surface structures of the native and target languages, rather than by "encouraging" the student to produce deviant utterances according to his current hypothesis until such time as he has had sufficient experience to correct himself. In free interaction we cannot ensure that sufficient opportunities of miscomprehension will occur at particular points of overgeneralization to provide the student with adequate data for the correction of his hypotheses. Nor can we ignore the factor of attention. The student attending specifically to problems of comprehending and expressing his meaning comprehensibly may well not have sufficient cognitive processing capacity available to note and store at the same time signals of the deviancy of certain surface structure features. Inconvenient facts of this type seem to be easily forgotten as soon as we begin to explore again the attractive hypothesis that processes of learning a second language are identical with those for learning a first language. As Stern has put it so aptly: "Once language development has taken place, it produces a lasting structural change. If a new language is learned in later years, it is filtered through the language acquisition device of the individual, modified by his first language."[20]

Unfortunately for the "natural" language-learning argument, recent research has left it far from clear how the child does acquire his first language and some assumptions reflected in current writings on foreign-language teaching appear now to have very problematic status. Many foreign-language teachers seem not to be aware of the fact that very reputable linguists,[21] philosophers,[22] and psychologists have sharply criticized Chomsky's theory of an innate linguistic faculty which enables the child to identify the form of the grammar of the language by which he is surrounded. Schlesinger comments: "There can be no question, of course, that the organism comes to any learning task with some innate equipment; the question is only how much is innate. The soundest approach seems to be to make as few assumptions as possible, and to try to explain with these as much as possible." Bruner says, "I am prepared to believe that in the linguistic domain the capacities for categorization and hierarchical organization are innate and so, too, are predication, causation, and modification."[23] Braine would accept as innate the mechanisms which permit us to perceive temporal position and cooccurrence relations.[24] Ervin-Tripp observes that "order relations seem very apparent to children ... Order is almost always accurately reproduced in imitations."[25] Bever maintains that "there is not as much innate structure to language as we had thought, if the 'universal grammar' is stripped of those aspects that draw on other psychological systems" (notably mechanisms of perception, learning, and cognition).[26] The present consensus appears to be that it is the logical structures basic to various intellectual processes which are innate, and which distinguish man as a species, not language-specific structures, and that it is these logical structures which make it possible for man to acquire and use language as well as to perform other cognitive operations. In this sense the concepts of "noun phrase," "verb phrase," or "sentence" would not be innate, as McNeill had earlier suggested,[27] but rather the capacity to categorize, to establish hierarchies of categories and relations between categories, the categories themselves being derived from common experiences of man in a human environment. In this sense, foreign-language teachers have always exploited the innate language-related capacities of the students by taking for granted that they can apprehend basic relationships of temporal order, cooccurrence, category, and hierarchy, and such operative relations as agent-action, action-object, causation, and modification.

Even the Chomskyan concept of the child acquiring a language system by hypothesis-testing is by no means uncontested. Braine argues convincingly that the child cannot be proceeding by the testing of hypotheses because real hypothesis-testing is dependent on the reception of both positive information (acceptance) and negative informa-

tion.[28] Without negative information, that is, correction or
rejection of unacceptable sentences, a child cannot test
hypotheses about grammaticality. Yet, strong evidence exists
that children do learn language from positive information
only, even though some of this information is inaccurate
(e.g., in cases where the child's deviant utterance is accepted
by the adult). Whether children are corrected or not[29] they
acquire the language of the community in which they are
growing up, and busy parents notoriously miss many opportunities to correct their children's speech, even adopting the
children's own forms on occasions, forms which the child is
often hearing also from other children of his own age. We
also know that children do not adjust their utterances when
negative information is provided (even when this is done in
an insistent fashion, as with Braine's child at the beginning of
this paper)[30] but they continue to operate within their own
structural system until it has evolved to the stage where the
particular adjustment indicated by the correction becomes
functionally warranted. It is, therefore, far from proven that
the child acquires his first language by a process of
hypothesis-testing. We may like to use this technique in our
classes for motivational reasons or to add variety to our
approach but we cannot claim at present that it is more than
a heuristic on our part.

We are also told frequently these days that children do
not learn language from a limited and structured corpus, that
children hear language of all levels of complexity, and that it
is because of this constant exposure to a full array of
language structure and vocabulary from the beginning that
the child is able to discover for himself the complete
grammar of the language. Some people have asserted on the
basis of this presumably scientific information that second-
language students should not be presented in the early stages
with a simplified form of the language (that is, with basic
patterns and a limited vocabulary)[31] but be exposed from
the beginning to the full range of language.[32] More recent
child language acquisition studies have shown, however, that
it is not the case that the child learns from a wide variety of
complicated structures and vocabulary. Actually, the child
tunes out much of what he does not understand in language

which is not addressed to him. Attention and memory play essential roles in comprehension. What the child is not attending to is processed minimally, if at all, and the child's memory span initially is very short. The sentences to which he is directly exposed tend to be short, repetitive, and quite limited in range of structures and vocabulary. This we know from recent investigations of Ervin-Tripp and her associates at Berkeley. Ervin-Tripp quotes a sample of adult speech to a two-year-old child which runs as follows: "Come play a game wit' me. Come play a game with me. Wanna play a game with me? You wanna play a game with me . . . ? Come look at Mamma's colorin' book. You wanna see my coloring book? Look at my coloring book. Lookit, that's an Indian, huh? Is that an Indian? Can you say Indian?"[33] (The same mother was using with adult friends sentences like the following: "It gives me a certain amount of consolation which allows me to relax my mind and start thinking intelligently an' putting my efforts all in one y'know force goin' in one direction rather than jus' y'know continually feeling sorry for yourself.")[34] As for the child himself, Weir has given examples of the speech of her child, David, at three years of age, talking into the microphone with which he had become familiar: "Here's de place. Bad boy bad boy Dave. Bad boy bad boy Dave. Dave is not a bad boy. Mike is a bad boy. Dave is OK but Mike is not."[35] Here we have the child saying over to himself simple noun phrases with modifiers and affirmative and negative declarative sentences with occasional ellipsis.

We must at the present time be extremely wary of basing what we do in the foreign-language classroom on presumed definitive statements about language learning from either linguistics or psychology. As Schlesinger has put it so aptly: "Psychological theorizing about language learning is in its infancy, and generative grammar is not yet fast frozen."[36] Generative grammar is in fact in such a state of evolution at the moment[37] that we bystanders would do well to wait till the dust settles before attempting to shape our classroom practice in any radical way according to principles and structures which tomorrow may be *passé*. Lamendella has concluded that "theories of linguistic description are relevant

to language teaching only to the extent that they form part
of the data which psycholinguists may use in constructing a
cognitive theory of language. It is this theory which may
properly be utilized as the theoretical basis for second-
language pedagogy."[38] Such a theory of language stemming
from psycholinguistics is not yet in sight. As eminent a
cognitive psychologist as Bever observes: "I have said little
about the effects of general principles of learning on
linguistic structure because I do not know anything about
how language (or anything else) is learned, while I do have
some initial understanding of the mechanisms of perception."[39] Problems of first-language acquisition aside, there
are important discoveries in the area of perception, both
auditory and visual, which can help us to help our students
learn more efficiently and which can give us firmer bases for
the designing of learning materials. A little later we shall see
what light they throw on particular learning problems with
which we are all familiar.

There are, of course, cognitive psychologists who are
interested in both problems of learning in general and in
language learning. Carroll has quite a deal to say about both
in "Current Issues in Psycholinguistics and Second Language
Teaching",[40] where he deplores the misinterpretation of his
1965 article[41] in which he had discussed audiolingual habit
theory and what he had called cognitive code-learning theory.
In his 1971 article he calls for a "meaningful synthesis,"
suggesting that "if it does not seem too flip to do so," we
should call this approach "cognitive habit-formation theory."
This article should be read carefully by all those interested in
present controversies. Hebb, Lambert, and Tucker have
shown recently how Hebb's cognitive learning theory can be
applied to language learning.[42] Piaget has devoted his life's
work to the relationship between learning and cognitive
growth, and Bruner has made cognitive theory accessible to
teachers in "Toward a Theory of Instruction."[43]

At this stage, a word of warning. We hear a good deal
these days about a "cognitive" approach to foreign-language
teaching and its proponents speak as though the techniques
they propose in some way exemplify the principles of

cognitive psychology. When we examine what they are saying a little more closely we sometimes find that they are merely proposing a return to the deductive presentation of grammar rules before practice to make what is practiced presumably more "meaningful" and that this is considered a more "cognitive" way to proceed. I do not intend to consider here the pros and cons of a deductive versus an inductive approach. Kelly traces this controversy back at least to St. Augustine and quotes Lubinus in 1550 as writing: "Now what and how monstrous an absurdity is it . . . to bid them give an account, why they speake Latine right, before they can in any wise speake properly."[44] In a teaching situation both induction and deduction may be very effective depending on the way they are integrated into the total teaching-learning situation. In fact most teachers use one approach or the other at different times, depending on the age and ability of the learners and the nature of the problem under consideration. I am merely concerned here with the very meagre interpretation of cognition which identifies it with a deductive presentation of grammar rules and an emphasis on analysis of structure, useful as these may be at the right place and time. Psychologically speaking, analysis is a cognitive process but so, most definitely, is analogy, requiring as it does the prior recognition of a pattern—the realization that there is something in common between two otherwise different events, which is a process of abstraction. Learning rules is a cognitive process but so is inferencing. We cannot imitate without activating a cognitive process.[45] It is noteworthy that small children find it difficult to imitate an utterance: they either interpret and rephrase it, or they answer a question or perform an action.[46]

A cognitive psychologist would make no attempt to establish a value hierarchy for these processes. He tries to find out what takes place when we perform any of them. He is interested in different strategies of learning and the stages of maturation at which each becomes dominant, or is, in Piaget's system, at least a possible operation for the child. He is interested in how we recognize phonic or graphic patterns and the interpretations we impose upon them. He is interested in short- and long-term memory. He is interested in what makes any object of learning or any situation meaningful to a particular student. Essentially he is interested in what goes on *inside* the organism: how we observe, interpret, interrelate and comprehend, reorganize and use *any* material for learning, because all living is learning. From what he discovers he is able to make suggestions for improving institutionalized learning (that is, in-school tasks), recognizing that no process or procedure is appropriate for all types and conditions of learning.

For the cognitive psychologist, then, cognition "refers to all the processes by which the sensory input is transformed, reduced, elaborated, stored, recovered, and used . . . Given such a sweeping definition, it is apparent that cognition is involved in everything a human being might possibly do; that every psychological phenomenon is a cognitive phenomenon."[47] This processing of input and preprocessing of output is what we need to understand if we are to teach a foreign language. It is here precisely that we have much to learn from the experimental findings of the psychology of perception which has made great strides in recent years. Psychology is not an alien science coming to strange conclusions which contradict what we ourselves observe. Much of what the psychologist discovers appears to us to be "common sense" because he is describing the operations of the human organism. Thus recent psychological studies in perception help us to understand experiences enshrined in such familiar expressions as: *he was only listening with half an ear,*[48] *it was just on the tip of my tongue,*[49] *you took the words right out of my mouth,*[50] and *you can tell he's French by his accent.*[51]

I shall now take two common problems of foreign-language learning and show how recent theories of perceptual processing can help us to analyze and deal with them.

A teacher may ask: *If listening is a passive or receptive skill, why do students sometimes seem to hear what was never said?*

Studies in perception make it clear that listening is far from being a passive skill, and the same may be said of reading (which shares with listening certain processes in a different sense modality).[52] Listening involves an active cognitive processing. Far from being an act of reception it involves the construction of a message from phonic material, with the result that the message we construct may sometimes be different from the message the speaker intended. There are three stages in the aural reception of a message and changes in the original message can occur at each stage. First, the listener must recognize in phonic substance sound patterns in bounded segments related to phrase structure (here we are helped by the rhythm of speech). At this stage we are dependent on echoic memory which is very fleeting. Unless we interrelate meaningfully the segments we detect we lose them as echoic memory fades. To extract a message, then, we must immediately begin processing, identifying the groupings we have detected according to the content of our central information system, that is, according to knowledge we have already stored. (This store of knowledge is, of course, limited at first in the foreign language, but expands as we continue to learn.) We recirculate this organized material through our immediate memory thus building up an auditory memory of it which helps us retain the segments we are processing. It is valuable, then, for the language learner to recapitulate mentally what he is hearing as he processes its meaning (this is a form of subvocal matching). Much of this processing of incoming information takes place during the pauses in speech, so speech which has been speeded up within segments is still comprehensible if the pauses are slightly lengthened so that the overall presentation rate remains the same. There are implications here for presentation of listening comprehension materials on tape, especially in view of the modern emphasis on normal rate of speech from the early stages.

It should not surprise us that when we are listening to a language with which we are not very familiar we often lose whole segments here and there even though we comprehended them when they were uttered. At this stage we must interrelate incoming segments with those we have retained and hold some in immediate memory to interrelate them with what follows, so that we can construct a sequential meaning for the utterance and for the sequence of utterances. We are then, by our organization, anticipating the full form of the message, and this explains why we often supply a completion when the speaker hesitates. The more we can gather the incoming information into meaningful chunks[53] the more we can retain. It is therefore important to train students in the perceiving of groups of words as units. To achieve this we should encourage our students to repeat what they hear in meaningful segments, and we should ask questions which require meaningful segments, rather than single words, as answers. It is also important to train students to hold longer and longer segments in their memory to improve comprehension.

Having constructed *our* meaning from what we are receiving, we recode this for long-term storage, that is, we reduce it to the "gist," and this is what we recall when asked about it. When we ask students questions about what they have been hearing, we should always encourage them to give the answers in their own words in the foreign language rather then expecting them to repeat exactly what they heard. This encourages real processing rather than superficial "playback," and gives practice in retrieval of the coded material.

It is clear from this analysis that attention plays an important role in comprehension. If attention wavers, we identify the wrong segments, we skip some segments, and we construct a different, idiosyncratic message. We know also that reinforcement plays a role in maintaining attention, so listening should be accompanied by some activity through which the student can demonstrate his comprehension and experience the pleasure of success. If he can do this through some form of personal expression in speaking or writing, the student learns at the same time that comprehension of a message is part of a communicative act. Set is also a significant factor. We hear what we expect to hear. In normal communication the context (the situation, the time of day, the persons interacting) helps us in interpreting a message. If we miss a segment or two, or if some of what we have heard "slips our mind," we fill in the gaps from expectations based on previous experience in such situations. This is why listening comprehension is facilitated when there is a visual or situational element, or even some background noises on the tape to indicate that the speakers are in a railroad station or at the seaside.

Emotion affects our cognitive processing. Personal thoughts and apprehensions take up some of the limited processing capacity, interfering with interpretation and retention of what is being perceived. It is natural, then, that the nervous or embarrassed student cannot "hear" well, or "hears" what was never said. The more disconcerted he becomes the more he grabs at semantic clues here and there and tries to process some kind of message. It is also natural for a student to forget what he heard and understood, and be unable to recount it. Material which is relatively unfamiliar cannot be gathered into large enough chunks, processing capacity is overstrained, and there is not enough cognitive energy left for the listener to rehearse and recode for storage what is being interpreted. In this case the student understands as he hears each segment but cannot store a sequential message.

For our second problem we imagine our teacher complaining:

My students rattle off drills (or write out paradigms; or whip through packets) all right, but they never seem to remember anything from one day to the next.

How familiar this sounds! These students are relying on short-term memory for their answers, particularly in drills and exercises where all the elements are supplied. In aural-oral drills particularly, the rhythm of the cues helps the students to produce the answers with a minimum of cognitive processing. Since they are not personally identifying the salient regularities in the material they are "rattling off" they are not forming concepts which they can relate to other information in the long-term store. Each utterance is a relatively unrelated new experience. Once a concept is formed, each utterance in a series becomes a variation on a theme which permits rehearsal and recirculation of the concept for recoding in long-term memory. Sentences in most drills and exercises are semantically empty for the student in the sense that they have no personal reality for him as a reflection of his present experience: they become exercises in manipulation of language segments which is purposeful only as manipulation. Mechanical, nonmeaningful activity does not use up a great deal of processing capacity— just enough to imitate, more or less accurately, and make minor adjustments. As a result a process of *time-sharing* takes place on the following pattern:

> *je mange du fromage* . . .
>> (That boy with the red hair looks interesting.)
> *je mange des pommes* . . .
>> (He's drumming rhythmically with his fingers.)
> *je mange des carottes* . . .
>> (I wonder if he likes dancing.)
> *je mange de la viande* . . .
>> (Ah! he prefers cinnamon gum.
>> I must remember that.)

It is no wonder, then, that the point of the drill never reaches the long-term store from which it could have been retrieved the next day or a week or two later.

Other problems which I would like to have considered, had the time allowed, are the following:

We've practiced and practiced that structure but they still get it wrong when they try to say something on their own.

Mary's the first to recognize when something is wrongly pronounced, yet her own pronunciation is nothing to write home about.[54]

They say every sentence we utter is one that's never been heard before. Most conversations don't sound that original to me.

And finally one remark I heard recently at a discussion on individualized instruction:

Where do all these paragons come from who go off in a corner by themselves and work like mad? I know mine would just goof off!—which brings us into the whole area of the psychology of motivation![55]

Carroll observes that "the 'new orthodoxy' in linguistics and psycholinguistics has made certain statements that have made second language teachers almost despair of their

profession."[56]   Teachers, he says, need to be constantly
reminded of practices that "have long been the property of
good language teachers, from the days of Gouin, de Sauzé,
Palmer, Sweet and other pioneers . . . because they tend to
develop, under the pressure of new fads and theories, a kind
of professional panic and anxiety about their work."[57] The
busy teacher, exhilarated or wearied by a long day working
with impatient and ebullient students, hardly needs to read:
"that people can learn, is an undeniable fact of life; that
people can teach, is an interesting hypothesis, but unsubstan-
tiated."[58] As a witticism it is worth recalling for the next
faculty meeting, but as teachers we realize it is mere playing
with words. It is based on a view of teaching (the teacher as
authority figure)[59] which is by no means axiomatic. That
teachers are "managers of the learning process"[60] is equally
authoritarian. It is time to return to the concept of teaching
which Dewey expressed so aptly in 1897 (the tradition is, of
course, even older): "the child's own instincts[61] and powers
furnish the material and give the starting point for all
education. Save as the efforts of the educator connect with
some activity which the child is carrying on of his own
initiative independent of the educator, education becomes
reduced to a pressure from without[62] . . . The teacher is not
in the school to impose certain ideas or to form certain habits
in the child but is there as a member of the community to
select the influences which shall affect the child and to assist
him in properly responding to these influences."[63] With this
concept of teaching, we select, from among practices we
know, those which are appropriate to the various aspects of
language acquisition, refining them in accordance with theory
and experience.

The simple answer to the problem is not merely "individualization." An individualized program, just as much as a
classroom situation, presupposes materials with built-in learning approaches. Without guidance students may work in ways
which are quite inefficient for language acquisition, just as an
uninformed teacher may work inefficiently in class. Analyses
of problems like those above show the types of useful
indications we as teachers can gain from an understanding of

cognitive processes—information that will help us to understand the problems of individual students and to design materials and activities with which they will be successful because we are not demanding of them responses which are beyond their processing capacities at a particular stage. If teachers are to be required more and more to prepare or adapt materials themselves as individualization becomes more widely accepted as an approach to school learning, they will need to think carefully about how students learn and arrange the conditions and "select the influences" accordingly. To quote a famous poet: "Men must be taught as if you taught them not."[64]

FOOTNOTES

[1]M. Braine, "On Two Types of Models of the Internalization of Grammars," in Dan I. Slobin, ed., *The Ontogenesis of Grammar* (New York: Academic Press, 1971), pp. 160-61.

[2]Example cited in Susan Ervin-Tripp, "Structure and Process in Language Acquisition," in James E. Alatis, ed., *Bilingualism and Language Contact: Anthropological, Linguistic, Psychological, and Sociological Aspects,* Monograph Series on Languages and Linguistics No. 23 (Washington, D. C.: Georgetown University Press, 1970), p. 340.

[3]Gilbert A. Jarvis says, "In the present sense of the term, we shall have to get 'teachers' out of our schools and replace them with facilitators—facilitators of learning." See "Individualized Learning—Where Can We Risk Compromise?" in *Modern Language Journal*, 4 (1971): 376.

[4]R.L. Cooper, "What Do We Learn When We Learn a Language," *TESOL Quarterly*, 4(1970): 312. In this article Cooper has provided us with a number of interesting insights into language learning. I have extracted from it the particular sections quoted because in them Cooper has described in a succinct fashion a particular viewpoint which I wish to analyze and discuss.

[5]Notably in *Aspects of the Theory of Syntax* (Cambridge: MIT Press, 1965); *Cartesian Linguistics* (New York: Harper and Row, 1966); and *Language and Mind* (New York: Harcourt, Brace and World, 1968).

[6]"Possible" in the sense that it is congruent with the particular form of innate equipment with which each human being is endowed and is, therefore, a language of a type which a human being can learn naturally.

[7]Chomsky, *Aspects*, p. 25.

[8]Chomsky, *Language and Mind*, p. 76.

[9]Ibid.

[10]For a full description of LAD see D. McNeill, *The Acquisition of Language*: *The Study of Developmental Psycholinguistics* (New York: Harper and Row, 1970), pp. 70-71.

[11]Chomsky, *Aspects*, p. 30.

[12]V. J. Cook, "The Analogy between First and Second Language Learning" in *IRAL* 7(1969): 216. After examining the research on first language acquisition of the mid-sixties, Cook sets out four requirements which would need to be met by a method of teaching foreign languages which could claim to be based on these theories. The suggestion taken up by Cooper is one of these requirements. Cook concludes: "No method can at present claim to fulfill these requirements. It remains to be seen whether they can in principle be fulfilled, whether, in fact, the analogy of first and second language learning is sound."

[13]Cooper, pp. 312-313.

[14]Chomsky, *Aspects*, p. 53.

[15]McNeill (1970), p. 36.

[16]Cooper, while claiming that "first and second language learning are analogous" and that a second language is not "learned in any fundamentally different way than a first language," nevertheless lists some of the "cognitive differences" in the two situations. "In spite of these differences," he says, "there seems to be little evidence that the actual language-learning *processes* differ for the child and the adult." In the present state of knowledge I would say that there is very little evidence either for or against such a conclusion because there has not been to date a great deal of experimental research into the specific language learning processes of the adult. The question is, therefore, still an open one.

[17]In "The Arbitrary Basis of Transformational Grammar," *Language*, 48 (1972): 76-87, George Lakoff says: "The theory of generative semantics claims that the linguistic elements used in grammar have an independent natural basis in the human conceptual system . . . In generative semantics, possible grammars are limited by the requirement that the nonphonological elements used have a natural semantic basis, independent of the grammar of any particular natural language" (pp. 77-8).

[18]Roar Ravem, "Language Acquisition in a Second Language Environment," *IRAL*, 6 (1968): 175-85.

[19]Jack C. Richards, "Error Analysis and Second Language Strategies," *Language Sciences*, no. 17 (October, 1971): 12-22.

[20]H. H. Stern, "First and Second Language Acquisition" in *Perspectives on Second Language Teaching*, Modern Language Center Publications No. 1 (Toronto: The Ontario Institute for Studies in Education, 1970), p. 64.

[21]As an example, see Ernst Pulgram, Review Essay on Noam Chomsky, *Language and Mind*, *Modern Language Journal*, 55(1971): 474-80.

[22]See Nelson Goodman, "The Emperor's New Ideas" in S. Hook, ed., *Language and Philosophy* (New York: New York University Press, 1969), pp. 138-42.

[23] J. Bruner, "On Cognitive Growth" in J. Bruner et al., *Studies in Cognitive Growth* (New York: Wiley, 1966), p. 43.

[24] Braine, p. 171.

[25] Ervin-Tripp, p. 335.

[26] T. G. Bever, "The Cognitive Basis for Linguistic Structures" in J. R. Hayes, *Cognition and the Development of Language* (New York: Wiley, 1970), p. 352.

[27] McNeill, pp. 70-71.

[28] Braine, pp. 155-68.

[29] E. Lenneberg says that even "children suffering from gross and criminal parental neglect" learn to speak the language of their community, in "A Biological Perspective of Language" in E. Lenneberg, ed., *New Directions in the Study of Language* (Cambridge: MIT Press, 1964), p. 67.

[30] For a similar example see D. McNeill, "Developmental Psycholinguistics" in *Genesis of Language*, F. Smith and G. A. Miller, eds., (Cambridge: MIT Press, 1966), p. 69.

[31] See L. A. Jakobovits, "Psychological Perspectives on Individualized Foreign Language Instruction" in H. Altman and R. Politzer, eds., *Individualizing Foreign Language Instruction* (Rowley, Mass.: Newbury House, 1971), p. 94.

[32] See L. A. Jakobovits, *Foreign Language Learning: A Psycholinguistic Analysis of the Issues* (Rowley, Mass.: Newbury House, 1970), p. 25.

[33] Ervin-Tripp, "An Overview of Theories of Grammatical Development" in Slobin, p. 194.

[34] Ibid.

[35] R. Weir, "Some Questions on the Child's Learning of Phonology", in Smith and Miller, p. 162.

[36] I. M. Schlesinger, "Production of Utterances and Language Acquisition" in Slobin, p. 100.

[37] Here I am referring to the active controversy between "classical" transformation-generative grammarians who are further developing Chomsky's system and the generative semanticists like Lakoff and McCawley who have an affinity with case grammarians like Fillmore. Lakoff tends to the view that what is innate and universal is an apprehension of logical categories and meaningful relations rather than abstract syntactic principles of a potential language. The various linguistic schools of thought have provided interesting (and often unexpected) insights into the way language operates. These we should draw on in constructing teaching materials and in helping students learn language, but we should use caution at the moment in making definitive statements about language learning based on one particular theory rather than another.

[38] J. T. Lamendella, "On the Irrelevance of Transformational Grammar to Second Language Pedagogy," *Language Learning*, 19 (1969):270.

[39] Bever, p. 350.

[40] J. B. Carroll, "Current Issues in Psycholinguistics and Second Language Teaching," *TESOL Quarterly*, 5(1971): 101-14.

[41] J. B. Carroll, "The Contributions of Psychological Theory and Educational Research to the Teaching of Foreign Languages," *Modern Language Journal*, 49(1965): 273-81.

[42] D. O. Hebb, W. E. Lambert, and G. R. Tucker, "Language, Thought, and Experience," *Modern Language Journal*, 55(1971): 212-22.

[43] Cambridge:The Belknap Press of Harvard University Press, 1966.

[44] For a full discussion of the induction-deduction controversy down the ages, see L. Kelly, *25 Centuries of Language Teaching* (Rowley, Mass.: Newbury House, 1969), pp. 34-43. Lubinus quotation p. 37.

[45] Ervin-Tripp, p. 316, states that "at a minimum, it can be shown that imitation requires perception, storage, organization of output, and motor output. In addition, before the storage phase there will be interpretation if the material is interpretable." See also Hebb, Lambert, and Tucker, p. 218.

[46] Ervin-Tripp, p. 317.

[47] U. Neisser, *Cognitive Psychology* (New York: Appleton-Century-Crofts, 1967), p. 4.

[48] Discussed in Ervin-Tripp, p. 317.

[49] See "The 'Tip of the Tongue' Phenomenon" in Roger Brown, *Psycholinguistics* (New York: The Free Press/Macmillan, 1970, pp. 274-301. Originally published 1966.

[50] For further information on this phenomenon see Article 7, "Linguistic and Psychological Factors in Speech Perception and Their Implications for Teaching Materials."

[51] See Ervin-Tripp, p. 323.

[52] Both listening and reading are discussed at length in Article 7 in this book.

[53] This term was used by G. A. Miller in his famous article "The Magical Number Seven, Plus or Minus Two: Some Limits on our Capacity for Processing Information," *Psychological Review* 63 (1956):81-96.

[54] As well as the processes outlined in note 45 for imitation, the student's own production of sounds when speaking is dependent on articulatory skill and kinesthetic feedback which vary from individual to individual so that the student's internal representation of the sound may not be reflected accurately in his production. Students also vary in their inhibitions about making "strange" sounds or in adopting these sounds as a permanent form of expression. Also during production other factors are competing for the limited processing capacity of the individual. For a full discussion, see Ervin-Tripp, pp. 316-26.

[55] I have dealt with this aspect of psychology at length in Article 5, "Motivating through Classroom Techniques."

[56] Carroll, pp. 108-9.

[57]Ibid., pp. 112-13. It is interesting to note that Gouin referred to his method as "psychological" or "natural."

[58]Jakobovits, "Psychological Perspectives," p. 91.

[59]Ibid., p. 97.

[60]Report of the Committee on the Process of Contracting in Foreign Language Learning in Altman and Politzer, p. 123.

[61]Views on instincts have changed considerably since 1897, but the sense of the passage is clear and startlingly contemporary.

[62]John Dewey, "My Pedagogic Creed" (1897), reprinted in M. S. Dworkin, ed., *Dewey on Education* (New York: Teachers College Press, 1959), p. 20.

[63]Ibid., p. 24.

[64]Alexander Pope, *Essay on Criticism III*.

7

Linguistic and Psychological Factors in Speech Perception and Their Implications for Teaching Materials*

Speech perception, it must be admitted, is a subject about which very little is known with any certainty. How is it possible, we may ask, for a person to extract a message from a continuous stream of sound which trained phoneticians find difficult to segment when the acoustic signal is recorded on a spectrogram. Yet, despite linguists and psychologists, understanding utterances is the common experience of every normal human being, and despite our ignorance of its nature we continue to train students who can understand not only their native language but foreign languages as well.

There are many questions about speech perception for which at present we can expect no definitive answers. Some maintain that the reception of a message is determined by the operation in reverse of the same processes as those involved in its emission. For this view there is as yet little experimental evidence and some that would seem to refute it.[1] Others consider that we perceive an oral message by covertly constructing a parallel message with which we compare it for fit—if this is so, speech perception must be considered a

---

*This article reprinted from *The Psychology of Second Language Learning*, eds. Paul Pimsleur and Terence Quinn, (Cambridge University Press, 1971).

special case of speech production. Still others consider speech perception a distinctive process in which the decoding rules draw on different factors from the encoding rules of speech production, with semantic cues playing a predominant role. Most linguists have concentrated on the system of rules which must be internalized if speech production is to be a theoretical possibility and Chomsky at least sees no difference between the knowledge of the language which must be posited for hearing and for speaking. The model of such a system of rules is a description of competence with no pretence at describing performance.[2] Psychologists, on the other hand, must concern themselves with the behavioral reality of the systems of rules elaborated by linguists, attractive as these may be as theoretical models, and they cannot accept without experimental evidence identity of process in performance for the two aspects of the communication act. As applied linguists we are caught in the middle and for our practical purposes we may be led sorely astray if we accept a theoretical model as a representation of psychological reality without looking for experimental validation.

Many writers have classified the comprehension of speech as decoding, and left it at that. This term is deceptively simple for a process which involves first perceiving that there is a systematic message rather than accidental noise in a continuous stream of sound, then apprehending and identifying within this stream bounded elements (segments) which the listener has never heard in exactly this form before, each segment having a distinctive structure and combining with other segments within a more extensive organized system. As the listener seeks to interpret the message he is hearing, this structuring within and among segments requires that he retain elements he has already apprehended until their relationships with succeeding elements have been established, and that he then engage in a continuous readjustment of his interpretation of each developing structure in view of what has preceded and in anticipation of succeeding segments. The listener is thus engaged in a continuous process of analysis and synthesis, in which factors of attention and memory are vitally involved. Comprehending a message is not merely attending to a stream of sound and establishing some construction at the whim of the listener: there is a highly complex structured system involved which has an existence apart from this particular listener and speaker and which is known to varying degrees of complexity by both. Nor is comprehension the passive reception of an already structured message. Since the speaker and the listener in a communicative act are different persons whose competence in the language is never identical, it is quite possible for the message perceived to be structured differently from that intended by the speaker. With a message in a language which is not the native language of one of the two participants the discrepancy in competence may be considerable and the probability that the message perceived will be identical to the message emitted will be correspondingly reduced. The structure apprehended by the listener in the stream of sound will also be influenced by situational context and by such personal factors as set, fatigue, and emotion. As a result, the message one person finally receives will not correspond precisely to the message another person would have perceived in the same communication sequence. Listening comprehension is an area in which linguistic and psychological factors are inextricably interwoven and as a phenomenon it can never be explained purely from the point of view of the psychologist or of the linguist. Insofar as it is a performance phenomenon it can be investigated empirically as behavior (behavior involving two persons), but such investigation will be peripheral unless it takes into account what the linguist has to say about competence and the organization of the language system.

There is reason to believe that the act of perception is not a purely passive one. It is an act of construction rather than of reception.[3] In continually varying sounds we recognize a phonemic system: combinations of sounds with certain complexes of distinctive features which we have come to accept within a certain band of tolerance as sounds of the particular language to which we think we are listening. Should we anticipate that an utterance will be in a specific language, we will not perceive the same combinations of sounds as we would have perceived if we had been expecting

another language, although the sound signal itself will not
have changed. As we listen for a particular language we will
not be disconcerted by variations in sound sequences which
represent the same morphemes because we have internalized
a system of morphophonemic rules which enable us to adjust
our construction appropriately beneath the level of conscious
attention and effort—we are, however, 'hearing' the variants
even if these are not made distinctly because this is what
learning this language has made us expect.

Beyond this, we perceive in a continuous sound signal
units and groups of units which as yet no machine has been
able to identify consistently except when utterances have
been shaped to conform to certain restrictions which suit its
program. These segments are perceived by the listener as
belonging to groupings which possess a meaning at a deeper
level of analysis because of the categories to which we assign
the whole, and often parts, of each segment and because of
the interrelationships we perceive among these categories,
categorization extending to larger and larger internally
structured segments until the ultimate category of the
discourse itself is reached. The groupings we perceive form a
rhythmic pattern which helps us retain what has been
apprehended in earlier groupings long enough to interrelate it
with later groupings in such a way as to make the utterance
meaningful. When we know a language well, these rhythmic
groups seem to form a pattern of rise and fall of the voice in
harmony with meaningful content which may itself be a
construction of the mind, rather than an uncontestable
acoustic fact, as certain recent experiments seem to indicate.[4] Lieberman hypothesizes that it is meaningful content
which suggests to us an appropriate learned intonation
pattern in some cases so that we perceive what we expected
even when the speaker has deviated from what we had
anticipated.

We can detect in the process of perceptual construction
three stages which should be kept in mind in the designing of
teaching materials. The first stage, sometimes called 'sensing',
is a stage of rapid impressions, only roughly identified and
differentiated and is relatively passive and receptive. At this
stage we impose some rudimentary segmentation on what we

hear. We are dependent on echoic memory which is very fleeting (it has been estimated to last for a few seconds), so actual items heard are not long retained unless they are interrelated in some meaningful way with other items. The rapid synthesis of impressions which we form is a construction resulting from our familiarity with the phonemic system, the morphophonemic rules, and the broad syntactic categories. As a result, much of what we have actually experienced auditorily does not pass on to the second stage because in our first rapid selection we have rejected as 'noise' elements that did not fit in with our initial construction. These sensory items then pass from echoic memory and can have no further effect on our interpretation.

The second stage is one of identification through segmentation and grouping. We segment and group at various levels as we apply the phonotactic, syntactic, and lexical collocational rules of the language to which we are attending. This identification is not the identification of an input identical with that of previous auditory experiences, since what we are identifying we may never have heard in exactly that form before. It consists of an identification of configurations of attributes which distinguish categories, and then of wider categories of which the already identified categories are the attributes. In this way associations are aroused within the centrally stored information system. This identification process is an active, detailed one which processes the signal it is receiving sequentially, interrelating the segments it has already identified and those it is identifying within the phrase structure of the utterance. At this stage memory is still auditory, but because of the initial grouping in a rhythmic form which is tentatively meaningful, insofar as the phrase structure has as yet been apprehended, the auditory segments (or 'chunks' in G. A. Miller's terminology) are more easily retained.[5] It is because of this greater power of retention that we can suspend judgment where there is ambiguity of structure, holding perceived segments in our mind, ready to make the necessary adjustments as the form of the phrase structure becomes clear.

There is considerable discussion as to whether this process is one of analysis-by-synthesis. It seems difficult to explain the conversion of auditory information, received from outside the nervous system, into cognitive meaning. According to the analysis-by-synthesis hypothesis, as we listen we construct a parallel message within our own cognitive system, according to the organized rules we have internalized, and compare it for match, or fit, with what we are perceiving aurally. This hypothesis seems to tally with our common experience of supplying words when others pause, or of believing we are following with comprehension another person's message when suddenly we are disconcerted by the next element and have to revise our projection of the form of the utterance. The hypothesis is in some ways an attractive one, but as yet a satisfactory model of the process which could operate in real time has not been developed. Further, analysis-by-synthesis cannot explain common substitution errors. If the input on which our matching is based is an acoustic signal, then it should be impossible to 'hear' words which have not been uttered, yet this is a common experience springing from our projection of the probable form of the utterance to which we are attending. It seems plausible, therefore, that we are engaged as we listen in some form of anticipatory projection, with adjustive correction should the utterance not conform with our expectations. This projection is based on our familiarity with the phrase structure, morphology, and lexical collocations of the particular language to which we are listening, as well as the extra-linguistic factors of situation and gesture. The less familiar we are with these elements the more difficult we find it to comprehend and retain what we hear because of our inability to anticipate appropriately. The development of an adequate model of comprehension must, however, await more substantial knowledge of the actual processes involved from the psychological point of view.

Whatever may be the precise nature of the identification process, we would not remember what we had perceived were it not for the third stage, that of rehearsal and recoding of the material, which must take place before what we have perceived enters into long-term storage. (Although this is called here a 'third stage' it must be considered as taking place simultaneously with the ongoing interpretative process.) Rehearsal refers to the recirculating of material through our cognitive system as we relate it to what follows and at times readapt what we have already interpreted in what we have already heard. Without rehearsal the auditory material in the memory would fade very rapidly and we would not be able to follow the line of thought in an utterance or series of utterances. It seems, however, probable that we do not store the material exactly as we first perceived it; rather we recode it in a more easily retainable form. A number of experiments seem to support the hypothesis that long-term storage (after thirty seconds) is in deep structure form:[6] that is, that the material perceived is detransformed and the basic semantic information retained, perhaps with transformational markers which enable the listener to re-capture the original form if necessary. This hypothesis is consistent with common experience: when asked about what we have heard, we tend to give the gist of it, usually in simple active affirmative declarative sentences (which are referred to in the literature as SAAD). Such sentences are closest to base strings to which obligatory transformations only have been applied. It is optional transformations (such processes as passivization, nominalization, and self-embedding) which seem to be dispensed with for storage although the semantic markers of such transformations as affect meaning (e.g., question, negation) are retained in the base. A series of simple kernel-like utterances is more redundant than utter-ances with a number of transformations which combine information and this redundancy aids memory. Recoding for retention must be performed immediately and without conscious attention or the listener misses part of the next grouping while he is rehearsing the recoding of the preceding segments. It is through recoding that the listener clarifies interpretatively relationships between·what is being attended to and what has already been assimilated, and this establish-ing of meaningful associations is essential to storage and later recall.

At this point it is interesting to consider Fillmore's proposal that grammatical subject and object are surface features.[7] Real meaning is in the deep structure: not only the semantic contribution of the lexicon, but also the semantic aspect of syntactic relations. It is of interest that in psychological experiments on recall, the logical subject as expressed in an agent *by*-phrase has proved to be a more effective prompt than a nonagent *by*-phrase,[8] which seems to indicate the psychological reality of Fillmore's agentive and to give added support to the notion that information is stored in deep structure form.

The three stages in speech perception which have been described form in practice one complex operation. It is reasonable, however, to presume that the efficiency of the whole process will be increased if listening comprehension materials are so constructed that the student has specific practice in the various types of operations he must perform almost automatically in an integrated series if he is to comprehend speech at a normal speed.

It has sometimes been suggested that students should begin the study of a foreign language by being plunged into a 'bath' of foreign-language speech, that for some time they should listen only until they begin to absorb the language through continual exposure. (This has also been termed the 'sunburn' approach.) In the light of our analysis of the processes of speech perception, this method has little to recommend it. If the segmentation we make in the initial stages is vital, and if ready comprehension is to some extent dependent on our ability to project an anticipated message, then all that the 'sunburn' procedure can do is to familiarize the student to some extent with the general sound aura of the language, not the significant sound patterns, and encourage an attempt at segmentation based on native-language habits. It is our competence in the foreign language which enables us to segment and group meaningfully. Where the student does not as yet possess some degree of competence, he may be able to perform some rudimentary semantic decoding where mime and visual images are introduced to supply clues to meaning, but it is then not clear to what degree the student is merely decoding the visual or kinesthetic signal system. With this prop removed he may remember some precise associations of specific phrases but he will have learned little upon which he can later build a system of decoding.

It is hardly a great step forward, however, to suggest that listening comprehension will grow as competence in the language is established. We can do better than that.

The first stage of speech perception is one of rapid, fleeting impressions, crudely segmented before the echo of the stimulus has disappeared from the memory. The initial selection is vital and normally related to syntactic groupings. (Where the structure is complicated the listener may resort momentarily to the less certain ground of purely semantic decoding, which in its simplest form is based on the order of semantic elements and their probable relationships.) We can help the student at this stage by ensuring the prolongation of the auditory image.

In the early stages students should be encouraged to repeat to themselves the segments they have apprehended, first as stretches of sound, then in an attempt at syntactic grouping. The very effort of repetition forces the student to segment the stream of sound in some fashion, the auditory image is longer retained, and the student has time to relate segments and to readjust his developing interpretation. Experiments at Harvard have shown that speech can be speeded up within segments and still be comprehensible so long as the pause between segments which is essential for cognitive processing, is slightly lengthened, so that the actual rate of presentation is not increased.[9] The student should be trained to use the pause for conscious processing, until early segmentation has become automatic. Early listening comprehension materials should, then, be kept within the limits of structural patterns being learned, so that rapid identification of syntactic groupings is possible. Once the student has made an incorrect segmentation, he has lost the sound image and further adjustments must be made by conjecture and inference. Training in listening comprehension by parallel production is more than mere imitation: it forces concentration on segmentation as well as providing guided practice in the production of well-formed segments, thus integrating with listening comprehension an operation which is basic to creative speech production as well.

At the next stage, the student must identify more precisely and interrelate the segments he is holding in his short-term memory. Unless he is able to interrelate these meaningfully into larger groupings he will lose what he has so far retained. This is where the student will gain from systematic training from the beginning in the recognition of structural features. If he is ever to reach an advanced stage of listening comprehension where he can enjoy and later discuss all kinds of materials, he will need to be adept at rapid recognition of many indicators of structure. He must be able to categorize words and word groupings (in the practical sense of recognizing their function). He must be able to recognize rapidly sentence shape by identification of clues to question form, negation, coordination, subordination. He must recognize clues which indicate condition, purpose, temporal relationships. Such features are frequently signalled by initial words which should be apprehended immediately so that the mind can concentrate on less clearly marked syntactic relationships. He must be able to recognize rapidly signals such as prepositions, articles, and auxiliaries which help him discern constituents of phrase structure, and he must identify immediately—in order to discard them—prop words and hesitation words which add nothing to meaning but take up precious storage space (e.g., "vous voyez," "d'ailleurs," "effectivement;" "kind of," "you know," "I think"). Students should have frequent practice in repeating as units in meaningful contexts word groups of high frequency which contrast with those of their own language, and further practice in detecting these in listening materials. Exercises can be designed especially for practice in apprehending and matching orally certain types of structure (e.g., left-branching, right-branching, or nested constructions). Progressively developed these can be amusing exercises for laboratory practice. Once the student has been trained to listen purposefully and can identify readily the various clues to syntactic interrelationships which have been listed, his mind and memory will be free to concentrate on the lexical content of the message, using what he knows of reality to supply meaning when his knowledge of the foreign lexicon fails him.

Next there is recoding for retention. Here we may gain some ideas for teaching materials from the suggestion that information perceived aurally is detransformed for storage and is mostly recalled in simple active affirmative declarative sentences. We can aid the automatization of this process by giving students direct practice in such recoding. It is surface structure in the foreign language which is troublesome to the student because it is here that languages are differentiated and contrast. The student needs practice in detecting the main relationships (in Fillmore's terms the agentive, objective, instrumental, locative, among others); he needs training in abstracting these from the complications of the surface form and reducing the relationship extracted to a more basic form of expression: in other words he needs practice in giving the gist of what he hears in simple form. This he can then store, leaving his mind free to concentrate on incoming information. Exercises should be developed which force recognition of such deep structure relationships by using as prompt words for recall those which correspond to the agent, instrument, or objective. It is the deep structure relationships which constitute language universals and in the recognition of these relationships the student is able to draw on his cognitive abilities beneath the level of surface structure complications. Students should also be given exercises in which they are presented first with the essence of what they are to hear in basic, kernel-like sentences and are then required to listen to the same substance in more complicated form with numerous transformations. Students who are not trained to decode and recode in the foreign language will inevitably develop the habit of automatically converting what they hear into a simplified form in the native language, thus wasting much valuable time and energy in translation and retranslation and never developing speed and ease in direct comprehension.

One of the perennial problems in modern language teaching has been the development of fluent direct reading. Students have been trained to read fluently recombinations of foreign-language speech they have learned, and even carefully graded readers kept within specified limits of known vocabulary and structure, but when they are finally allowed to read less controlled materials it becomes apparent that they have not developed a technique for extracting meaning directly from the foreign-language text. Many fall back into mere translation; others adopt a predominantly semantic strategy, seizing on lexical elements they recognize here and there and constructing some garbled version which shows they have not understood the basic structuring of the meaning. Research into the act of reading for meaning has shown that the processes involved parallel those of listening comprehension: first, there is recognition in a fast impressionistic way of segments which for comprehension must be identified as meaningful segments of phrase structure; there is the necessity to interrelate these according to basic relationships, holding one segment in the mind and suspending judgment until other segments are identified and combined with it in a meaningful way.

There is the same need for rapid recognition of categories, of sentence shapes, of markers, of constituents of phrase structure and for penetrating beneath surface complications to basic relationships. In view of this similarity of processes, the teaching of fluent reading could be considerably facilitated by combining it with a program of training in listening comprehension. The effort at rapid segmentation (the identification of the essential relationships of the underlying phrase structure), the holding of chunks in the memory while awaiting confirmation of anticipations (that is, while waiting to see that the projected sentence is congruent with the actual sentence), the extracting of the gist (that is, the reduction to deep structure): all of these operations must be performed again in relation to the graphic medium. When the student is being trained in these specific operations for listening comprehension he should be made to realize their applicability to the other medium by being encouraged to read rapidly material based on the same content as what he has heard, and at other times to listen to oral presentations based on similar content to what he has read. The reading should not be done aloud, however, since hearing himself read and concentrating on how he is reading hinder the student in his rapid identification of the graphic symbol.[10]

Similar exercises to those outlined for listening comprehension should be developed for reading comprehension: reading the gist in simple active affirmative declarative sentences before reading a highly transformed version, practice in recounting in detransformed form what has been read, practice in detecting the deep structure relationships beneath the surface forms, rapid identification of cue words to structure and sentence shape. This is another whole area of concern and must be set aside for another time. All good teaching, however, is teaching for transfer (or, as in this case, transposition), and teaching of listening comprehension should be no exception.

FOOTNOTES

[1]I. M. Schlesinger, *Sentence Structure and the Reading Process* (The Hague: Mouton, 1968), Chapter 6.

[2]Noam Chomsky, *Aspects of the Theory of Syntax* (Cambridge: MIT Press, 1965). "To avoid what has been a continuing misunderstanding, it is perhaps worth while to reiterate that a generative grammar is not a model for a speaker or a hearer. It attempts to characterize in the most neutral possible terms the knowledge of the language that provides the basis for actual use of language by a speaker-hearer. When we speak of a grammar as generating a sentence with a certain structural description, we mean simply that the grammar assigns this structural description to the sentence. When we say that a sentence has a certain derivation with respect to a particular generative grammar, we say nothing about how the speaker or hearer might proceed, in some practical or efficient way, to construct such a derivation" (p. 9).

[3]For a full discussion with supporting experiments, see U. Neisser, *Cognitive Psychology* (New York: Appleton-Century-Crofts, 1967), Chapter 7.

[4]P. Lieberman, "On the Acoustic Basis of the Perception of Intonation by Linguists," *Word*, 21 (1965):40-54.

[5]G. A. Miller, "The Magical Number Seven, Plus or Minus Two," *Psychological Review*, 63 (1956):81-97.

[6]J. Fodor and M. Garrett, "Some Reflections on Competence and Performance" in J. Lyons and R. J. Wales, eds., *Psycholinguistics Papers: Proceedings of the 1966 Edinburgh Conference* (Edinburgh: Edinburgh University Press, 1966) pp. 148-51.

[7]C. J. Fillmore, "Toward a Modern Theory of Case" in David A. Reibel and Sanford A. Schane, eds., *Modern Studies in English—Readings in Transformational Grammar* (Englewood Cliffs, N. J.: Prentice-Hall, 1969), pp. 361-75.

[8]A.L. Blumenthal (1965), as described in R. J. Wales and J. C. Marshall, "Linguistic Performance," in Lyons and Wales, pp. 70-71.

[9]Harvard Center for Cognitive Studies: *Sixth Annual Report 1965-66*, p. 18; *Seventh Annual Report 1966-67*, pp. 30-31.

[10]Ibid., *Seventh Annual Report*, p. 32.

8

Foreign Languages in a Time of Change*

Recently, I have been reading a very interesting booklet—
the student evaluation booklet of a very well-known university—and I read some very provocative things in it. As
teachers we have been deploring the dropping of the foreign-
language requirement in many universities, but what does the
student say?

"As a foreign language requirement this course contains
all the necessary grammar and vocabulary except for
words of frustration, hostility, and anger. A good diction-
ary will fill in those educational gaps."

"(This course) ruins most students' averages, it ruins their
morale, it ruins their social life by staying in and studying
so much, and it really ruins any desire that any would
have to learn a foreign language."

As teachers we are bewildered by these reactions to our
carefully structured, well designed, pedagogically sound
programs. One student writes: "I sincerely urge you . . . . to
quit treating students as infants with your highly structured,
foolproof, unemotional (sequence)." So virtues become vices.

*Address given at the School-University Foreign Language Articulation Con-
ference at the University of Illinois at Urbana, October 28, 1971.

Yet we felt we were responding to the spirit of the times. Our students wanted emphasis on speaking rather than reading: didn't we give them that? No more silent classrooms: everyone could participate actively for thirty minutes out of thirty minutes. We provided them with the opportunity to work on their own with a "personal tutor" in the language laboratory. We gave them contemporary reading materials when they reached that stage. *What has happened to our students?* Where have we gone wrong? Does the fault lie with ourselves and our programs?

The title of this article is: "Foreign Languages in a *Time of Change.*" We may well ask: isn't every period a time of change? It has become a truism to say: Yes, but ours is a period of *rapid change.*

We have all heard of *culture shock*: it is the experience a person has in a foreign culture when suddenly all the familiar psychological cues that help him function in his own society are changed. In his new situation he has to ask himself how he should act and react to others, how he should time his actions, what is the correct social behavior. Why, he wonders, do these people seem indifferent to things which seem to him to be so important, even matters of principle. Everything in this new society is so strange and incomprehensible that he is disoriented and disturbed. In a recent book Alvin Toffler speaks of "future shock." "Future shock," he says, "is a time phenomenon, a product of the greatly accelerated rate of change in society. It arises from the superimposition of a new culture on an old one. It is culture shock in one's own society, but its impact is far worse."[1] He sees society at present as suffering from confusional breakdown.[2] *We* are caught in it; *our students* are caught in it: in a revolution in societal patterns, institutions, and values where familiar cues no longer provide a sufficient guide.

For us this is intensely confusing; for our students it is carrying them away from us fast in a developing pattern of new attitudes and values. Attitudinal changes which gradually evolved over a generation may now be effected within a decade. Unless we realize this and seek to understand these new attitudes and values the dislocation of our educational efforts will grow worse despite our well-meaning, even decisive, actions.

Many of us knew depression and war. We had to rebuild. We had to work hard, to delay gratification until we had achieved intermediate goals, to submit ourselves to years of discipline to attain the affluence we have today.

This generation is born with it and bored with it. This generation is the first in history that has a prolonged and leisured youth (as distinct from adolescence) with opportunities for intellectual, emotional, and moral development without the demands of societal responsibilities.[3] As the sociologists keep telling us, our young people are entering a post-industrial society in which many of the careers for which our generation had to prepare themselves with such assiduity will not exist (or will not exist in the forms in which we know them) when our students emerge from their prolonged youth to take their place in the larger society. To this generation, learning something to pass an examination as a passkey to career opportunities is meaningless. With "open admissions" we cannot even use acceptance into a college as a goad.

As Toffler has put it: "The technology of tomorrow requires not millions of lightly lettered men, ready to work in unison at endlessly repetitious jobs, it requires not men who take orders in unblinking fashion, aware that the price of bread is mechanical submission to authority, but men who can make critical judgments, who can weave their way through moral environments, who are quick to spot new relationships in the rapidly changing reality."[4] If as Postman and Weingartner have pointed out "a classroom is an environment and . . . . the way it is organized carries the burden of what people will learn from it,"[5] many foreign-language classrooms have been preparing students excellently for the demands of industrial as opposed to post-industrial society. Haven't we been teaching students to work in unison at endlessly repetitious tasks, and to take orders in unblinking fashion, with mechanical submission to authority?

The new society requires—

—men who can make critical judgments;

—who can weave their way through moral environments;

—who are quick to spot new relationships in the
   rapidly changing reality.

Where does foreign-language study fit into this new educational picture?

For Toffler it has no place at all. It is the first thing he eliminates. In his chapter, "Education in the Future Tense" we read: "Tens of millions of children today are forced by law to spend precious hours of their lives grinding away at material whose future utility is highly questionable. (Nobody even claims it has much present utility.) Should they spend as much time as they do learning French, or Spanish or German?"[6] Later he says:

> "Anyone who thinks the present curriculum makes sense
> is invited to explain to an intelligent fourteen-year-old
> why algebra or French or any other subject is essential for
> him. Adult answers are almost always evasive. The reason
> is simple: the present curriculum is a mindless holdover
> from the past."[7]

The attack is widespread. Toffler is only one voice. As foreign-language teachers we cannot put our heads in the sand. *Do we have an answer*? It cannot be a glib one; it must come from a careful study of the situation we are in.

Let us look, then, for further information. If our youth is passing through a revolution, what are the trends of this revolution? Here I would like to take up four illuminating observations of Professor Kenneth Keniston of the Department of Psychology at Yale. In an article: "You Have to Grow Up in Scarsdale to Know How Bad Things Really Are," he points to four trends in the thinking of our youth.[8] They are as follows:

> 1. A revulsion against the notion of quantity, particularly
> economic quantity and materialism, and a turn toward
> concepts of quality. (Keniston reminds us of the slogan of
> the French student revolt in 1968: "Long live the
> passionate revolution of creative intelligence.") This
> brings an emphasis on quality of experience, on the
> expressive, the aesthetic, the creative, the imaginative,
> even the fantastic.

2. A revolt against uniformity, equalization, standardization, and homogenization (against the "technologization of man") with the demand that individuals be appreciated not despite their differences but because they are different, diverse, unique, and noninterchangeable.

3. A continuing struggle against psychological or institutional closure or rigidity in any form, even the rigidity of a definite adult role, and the extolling of the virtues of openness, motion, and continuing human development. (Here we may think of the present resistance to requirements—any requirements.)

4. A revolt against centralized power and the complementary demand for participation. It is in this sense that students are demanding "relevance" in their educational program: a chance for the student to participate in his own educational experience in a way that involves all of his faculties, emotional and moral as well as intellectual.

Our highly structured system worked with another generation in another era. How can we meet the demands for quality of experience, for appreciation of difference, for openness and participation, while preparing people who can make critical judgments and face new relationships and new attitudes, even moral ones, without reactions of shocked withdrawal?

I think as foreign-language teachers we can, and I believe, moreover, that we should cease apologizing for our subject and trying to slip it in without people noticing, under the protective cloak of institutional requirements. *We do have something to contribute to the whole education of adolescence and youth*, but not by merely continuing to do as we have always done.

What do we need, then? Newer, more scientific methods that some guru is going to present to us in a neat package? It is certainly not new methods we need, but a new attitude: one that is less harassed and less pressure-bound by an earnest desire to teach more and more material. We need an attitude which allows the student to learn, that waits for the student to learn, that allows the student choices in what he shall learn.

In our earnestness, in our anxiety to do the best academically by our students, in the educational lag in our thinking which has carried over from the days when we had in our classrooms an elite, a chosen few, who pursued the esoteric study of a foreign tongue, we have structured and shaped learning experiences which have become homogenized and inflexible and have gradually eliminated (sometimes not so gradually) all but the fittest—those who seemed to us to fit best into the pattern of our often stereotyped advanced courses.

Now our students reject rigidity and structure, quantity of learning, and imposed experience. No wonder there is tension and often abrasive tension. In our concentration on how students learn a foreign language, we have forgotten *how students learn*. To quote Earl Stevick of the Foreign Service Institute: "We must no longer look at (the learner) only as 'linguistic man'—man regarded only as a potential internalizer and producer of alien sounds, words and patterns. Any language student is an entire social being."[9]

What have we, as foreign-language teachers, to contribute to our student's quality of life, to his development of critical and moral judgment, to his ability to adapt and readapt to changing attitudes and circumstances?

I think we are ideally suited to share in this function. Isn't ours the only subject which rudely thrusts the student into inevitable contact with other modes of thought and expression and forces him to think more critically about his own, and which also gives him vicarious experience in confronting and adapting to new ideas and attitudes? This is true only if we teach the foreign language with such an end in view, not, of course, if our sole aim is the drilling of irregular verbs and the mastery of the use of accents.

As I have said elsewhere in this regard:[10]

"The . . . . contribution of foreign-language study that is truly educational, in the sense that it expands the student's personal experience of his environment, and truly humanistic in that it adds a new dimension to his thinking is the opportunity it provides for breaking through monolingual and monocultural bonds. Such an experience reveals to the student that there are other ways of saying things, other values and attitudes than those to which his native language and culture have habituated him. Through this process he may develop new attitudes to ideas and peoples that will reduce his bondage to the familiar and the local while increasing his sympathy for persons of other cultures and languages. The new-generation student in our schools is internationalist and interculturalist in his aspirations; he is also brutally direct in demanding the rationale of what we are doing and what we are asking him to do. This basic contribution which foreign language can make to his development is one which he would welcome, but he must see that what we do in our classrooms really achieves such a purpose or he will drop out as soon as he conveniently may. If, as Harold Taylor has said: "The first task of education . . . . is to raise the level of awareness and response to *all* ideas, events, people, and objects,"[11] then foreign language taught with this end firmly in view can still claim that it has has a rightful place in the overall educational program of the school."

All this is very idealistic. What is the reality? Why do we find it so difficult to demonstrate this type of teaching in actuality?

Here we may listen to another student voice:

"Most people forget what they learned so soon after they've finished that even those who someday make it to Europe or South America can't use it. Besides, in this electronic age, the ideal of a multilingual Renaissance man is pitifully camp. You can travel farther and learn more about 'other cultures' on acid than on a world tour."

and again:

"too many books, too much stress on grammar, too little emphasis on their culture."

Are these complaints rather about the content than about the subject itself?

Perhaps we have been unable to get away in our thinking from the ideal, which comes from the days of selective high schools and privileged undergraduates, that all foreign-language students should be expected to attain near-native mastery of the language in all skills: an ideal which is impossible in the time available to us in most situations (and here I am not thinking of courses for foreign-language majors). We aim at near-native mastery for all and design our courses accordingly, then we leave up to eighty per cent of the students somewhere along the way, sometimes not very far. When they realize how little they know and how little they can use it, they become frustrated and hostile, and they grow into parents and community leaders opposed to such an experience for their children. How familiar this is to all of us! Can we realistically claim that *all* students need to attain this kind of language mastery?

We must decide what it is that we want every student to carry away even from one year's experience of foreign-language study. If it is a change in attitude and in his attitude to his own language and to language and communication as such—then we must design our program so that such an outcome is really achieved and evident. I submit that we have been giving too much thought to the formal structure of our programs while retaining the same old content: individualized instruction, computer-assisted instruction, writing behavioral objectives, systems approaches, or what you will, are still tailored to the present and future tense in Level One, the past and conditional tense in Level Two, the awesome subjunctive in Level Three.

At this point let me insert a warning. We cannot shift gears and move from an emphasis on skill-learning to the changing of attitudes without knowing something about the whole question of the effect of prior attitudes on the learning of controversial material; otherwise we may very well reinforce prejudices. We know that controversial material which fits in with our existing evaluative framework is readily retained whereas we tend to retain implausible material from the other side. In fact in their initial selection for retention from what we give them our students may misunderstand, distort, discount, or even reverse, in accordance with their own biases, the implications of what they are hearing, seeing, or reading.[12] Then if we limit ourselves to facts about a particular culture, these are very perishable, as we well know, and we may unwittingly be increasing the possibility of culture shock for our students when they encounter the realities, rather then helping them to understand what they see or hear. The attitude of the teacher who is dazzled and can see no wrong in the foreign culture can arouse rigidity and hostility. What we are out to develop is an openness to new ideas and new ways of expression and a tolerance of difference. We must learn how to achieve this.

What about the high percentage of our students (seventy or eighty percent in many cases) who will never be with us long enough to achieve mastery? Should we be honest and say we cannot give them anything which is worthwhile in the year or two they are with us? Or can we take a look at our programs and restructure them?

Here I am going to propose that whatever our situation: college, high school, junior high school, elementary school—wherever foreign-language study is begun—we design a two-stage program.

Stage One would be designed as terminal, designed so that whoever passed through it would have gained something of educational and humanistic value, even if he never studied a foreign language again in his lifetime. This would also be the stage for creating interest and enthusiasm in some, who would then wish to go on to Stage Two because they really wanted to master the language. Stage One would then be an end in itself and not merely the elementary stage of Stage Two, and certainly not *pre-* anything.

What would we aim for in Stage One? At the moment, I would say four things.

First: An introduction to language itself through a specific foreign language, gearing our study to the way language operations express meanings and the many ways meanings can be encoded; the way our language expresses our way of looking at things and the way another language expresses another people's way of looking at things. This study would be frankly contrastive.

For many years we have professed to be teaching our students to understand how language operates and to understand the operation of their own language better through the study of a foreign language. Most of this protestation has been lip-service. Are we really going to work out how to do this interestingly and significantly?

Second: an introduction to another people through language: the way another people thinks, feels, values, and acts in contradistinction to our own preoccupations, attitudes, and reactions. (This I have already written about at some length.)

Third: An experience of being another people, communicating as they do, acting as they do, relating as they do. Here our students learn the language and live the language. Language knowledge acquired is immediately acted out. Rules internalized become channels of communication. Practice in production is immediately incorporated into some form of authentic interaction.

Fourth: An experience of communicating with another people: speaking with them (where possible), writing to them, working and playing with them where a neighboring community makes this possible, sharing with them in joint or exchange projects (Here I would call your attention to a recent article of Dwight Bolinger of Harvard: "Let's Change Our Base of Operations" in the *Modern Language Journal* 25 (1971): 148-156.)

Methodologically we would aim at involvement of all students in planning, in group research and interaction, in interdisciplinary exploration, in human contacts in nearby communities or through correspondence.

Such a course would not be a waste of time for those who wished to master the language. It would foster attitudes which would carry them through the long, and often tedious, stages of disciplined language study. Our Stage Two students would not be a conscripted, but a self-selected, clientele with considerable experience in the area and an autonomous desire to do what they were doing.

I can already hear the old objections: Isn't this lowering standards? How are we going to test these courses across the board so as to satisfy administrators and parents? (For too long we have allowed the latter problem to hamstring our endeavors at realistic change.) There need be no "lowering of standards." Since the objectives will be different, we will expect different outcomes, a different type of achievement, and we will design different tests to conform with our objectives. We will expect to test, for instance, for certain understandings, for certain attitudes, for a new freedom we hope our students will have achieved. Such a test may very well mean no test at all in the conventional sense of the word. The present approach arouses hostility and frustration in many. Isn't it time, then, to consider new structures and a new content more congruent with the thinking and aspirations of the present generation of students?

Obviously such an approach will involve careful planning and preparing of materials, with perhaps pilot projects to work out the best way of proceeding. The present situation requires some intensive original thinking. As a profession, I believe we are capable of carrying such a project through.

I cannot dwell here on Stage Two which will be more akin to the language-learning situation to which we are accustomed. We would, however, now have a better motivated and a better prepared group, both from the point of view of linguistic awareness and cultural comprehension, a group which had chosen to study the language with the acknowledged purpose of seeking a high degree of mastery. What more could we ask for? Here I could say much about our need to shift gears too if we wish to conserve this group through the necessarily laborious period of developing comfortable competence of operation in the foreign tongue.

But let us not just talk or listen. Let us get down to some hard study and planning for the implementation of such a program.

FOOTNOTES

[1] Alvin Toffler, *Future Shock* (New York: Bantam Books, 1970), p. 11.

[2] Toffler, p. 343.

[3] This view is put forward by Kenneth Keniston, Department of Psychology, Yale University, in "You Have to Grow Up in Scarsdale to Know How Bad Things Really Are," *New York Times Magazine*, April 27, 1969, reprinted in *The University Crisis Reader*, vol. 2; *Confrontation and Counterattack*, eds. I. Wallerstein and P. Starr, (New York: Random House, 1971), pp. 453-68.

[4] Toffler, p. 402.

[5] N. Postman and C. Weingartner, *Teaching as a Subversive Activity* (New York: Delacorte, 1969), p. 18.

[6] Toffler, pp. 409-10.

[7] Toffler, p. 410.

[8]Keniston, pp. 464-65.

[9]E. Stevick, *Adapting and Writing Language Lessons* (Washington, D. C.: Department of State, 1971), p. 14.

[10]"Teacher-Student Relations: Coercion or Cooperation," Article 10 in this book.

[11]Quoted by A. E. Lean in *And Merely Teach* (Carbondale: Southern Illinois University Press, 1968), p. 58.

[12]D. Ausubel, *Educational Psychology: A Cognitive View* (New York: Holt, Rinehart and Winston, 1968), p. 390.

9

From the Pyramid to the Commune: The Evolution of the Foreign-Language Department *

The great monolith of the foreign-language department is splitting and cracking. Its foundation is disintegrating and falling away, or so it seems, and the effect is being felt right to the apex. Our beautiful aesthetically proportioned pyramid is threatened. Of course many of us haven't given too much thought to its lower structures for some time. We had our graduate students: our future professors with such fine minds (were there any others?). There were, of course, our majors, whom we regarded as potential graduate students, and then that lesser breed, the future secondary teachers who helped us pay our way. Were there a few minors? They obviously could not be serious or they would be majors. And that vast anonymous mass at the base in the service courses? Like the poor, they were always with us, for after all without the working poor how could an elite cultured class give its full attention to intellectual and aesthetic matters?

Paralleling this hierarchy of students we had our own inner core. At the apex were the senior professors, the scholars, concerned only with the elitist graduate student, preferably in thesis advisement on a one-to-one basis: the

*A paper presented at the Annual Meeting of the Association of Departments of Foreign Languages, Chicago, Illinois, December 26, 1971. Originally published in the *ADFL Bulletin* 3(1972): 13-17.

established scholar engaged with the most brilliant of the incipient scholars. Next came the aspiring younger faculty, the scholars of promise, interested only in the majors, and of these preferably the few destined for graduate study. Somewhat lower were our less scholarly, practical colleagues teaching teachers how and what to teach, and at the base the graduate assistants doing their time, poor souls, with the required courses, as we've all had to do in our day. No wonder there is alarm and consternation at the threat to the base: we cherish our antique monument as it is, because it memorializes in concrete form the glories of a past age.

Perhaps we need a new image for ourselves and for others. Instead of our well-proportioned pyramid, orderly and coherent, where each section fits into its place supporting the whole in anonymity and impersonality, we need a real community: a community of scholars, of learners at every level, in keeping with the true meaning of the word "scholar." I suggest that we renounce our historical monument and that we become a commune—an untidy, nonhierarchical, interacting, interdependent, evolving commune. And what shall we have in our commune? Plurality and diversification in unity, innovation and interaction in mutual tolerance and acceptance. In this way, if we are sincere in our conversion, we can provide for all types of students the truly humanistic experience which our discipline offers. We must renounce the idea that foreign-language study has a utilitarian value (although it may have for a few) and concentrate on developing people: interesting people who have read and experienced beyond the limitations of their own language and their own culture, flexible people able to react with equanimity to new ideas and ideals and to see them in perspective because of their wider experience in another culture and in another age. In this way what we have to offer can be of value to all who come to us no matter how short their stay and no matter what their future role.

Idealistic? Maybe. A little whimsicality will help us to take ourselves less seriously, and to worry less intensely, in this period of rapid change which is affecting, whether we will or not, our institutional role and our clientele. The new image I propose is not as fanciful as it may seem but its implications cannot be realized overnight. The establishment of our commune is not merely a question of breaking down caste and challenging authority structures. Of the latter there will always be some. Even in a commune natural leadership patterns evolve as events and necessity sort out the decision makers from the followers. The significant change must be in our attitudes within the community: in the development of a new acceptance of difference and a new appreciation of diversity of gifts and interests.

How, then, does our commune differ from our pyramid? First the monolith disappears—that monolith where each step is preliminary to the next and each leads on inevitably to the apex. Stop at one step and where are you? Nowhere in particular—merely somewhere on the way. Within the commune there is a plurality of tasks and achievements, each one a worthwhile accomplishment in itself. People come and people go; some stay, some leave, some return. Whenever they are within the commune they are fully participating members—they belong, they count, they are respected—for every contribution of effort and interest helps to create and maintain the commune. He who leaves takes away with him a complete experience, perhaps shorter and less intense than if he had stayed, but in any event not a partial experience that is merely anticipatory and unsatisfying in its incompleteness.

So much for our metaphors. Let us express them rather in terms of courses and student-teacher interaction to make them comprehensible and practical. We need courses at every level which provide for a diversity of interests and time-objectives, courses which have satisfying content in themselves and are not merely preliminary to some future experience. In this sense a fair proportion of our courses can be designed as "terminal," so that the student who completes the course but goes no further can take away with him a full and enriching experience, while the student who continues will find his later experiences facilitated and illuminated by what went before. The secret is in the approach we take when planning our courses. As we are forced to compete for student interest in an open market we will need more and more to conceive and plan our courses imaginatively and realistically with the interests of a diversity of students in mind. We can no longer afford to regard our lower level courses, for instance, as "elementary" and "intermediate" (the very words enshrine a preparatory concept). Thinking of them as preliminary courses we try to include in them all the grammar we think our future majors should know until our students gag with revulsion. We often withhold till the fourth semester any material that is intellectually stimulating and then provide snippets from various centuries, surely worthy when seen in their literary context but utterly boring to the naive literary student.

Does a terminal course, in my sense of the term, necessarily have to be a "review of the grammar," ensuring that the short-term student takes away a thorough picture of the workings of the subjunctive and the intricacies of the pronominal system? Is this what he will quote with pleasure when looking back on his undergraduate days? Surely we can provide a choice for our students: a preparatory diet for those who intend to continue and are willing to prolong an arduous apprenticeship for the promise of future mastery, and, paralleling this, a stimulating and provocative offering for those who will leave us at the end of the semester. When are we going to do some serious research into the amount of grammar a person really needs to know actively in order to comprehend, and the amount of concentrated learning required for him to be able to recognize the rest when he needs it in the context of interesting material? Recent psychological research in reading and listening shows that there is a significant heuristic element at work in comprehension. Shouldn't we set some of our best graduate students to finding out which aspects of language structure must be thoroughly assimilated and which can be deduced from our knowledge of setting and semantic associations (particularly in languages with a large commonality of outlook and cultural context)? Once we have substantial research evidence in this area we may find we can reduce considerably the grammar content in terminal courses and use our time, and our students' time, for the type of confrontation with ideas and attitudes which we recognize as one of the major educational contributions we can make to undergraduate education.

A language is a vehicle. What about content? Are all students, or even most, at the lower levels interested in learning the language in order to read the literature? For those who are we bring the literature to them, carefully selected in theme and development to interest and stimulate them intellectually, while still linguistically within their capacity of comprehension. Some, let us face it, are interested rather in current affairs and the preoccupations of their contemporaries in the other culture. For these why not use the newspapers and magazines of the day as the major course content? The interpretation of such contemporary documents will certainly challenge our understanding of present-day life and institutions and their roots in earlier periods. Some students are fascinated by the clash of attitudes, values, and behavior patterns between cultures: if so, we can provide opportunities for them to see the other culture and their own through foreign eyes—often a startling experience. Is it drama and film they seek? These we can provide. Should they wish to learn only to communicate, to comprehend and be comprehended, it should not be such a struggle for us to eliminate from our courses the written exercises they no longer need. If they wish only to read but not to discuss in the foreign language, surely this too is a legitimate interest. For far too long we have allowed a commendable obsession with fairness in grading to preoccupy us so that in order to ensure that all are rewarded alike we serve for all an identical, often insipid and tasteless diet which few enjoy.

For a plurality of student needs we must provide a plurality of content. But why not also a plurality of approaches? Once again with the best of intentions we have insisted that all be taught alike despite the differences in their learning patterns and the equally important differences in the natural instructional styles of their instructors. Here again uniformity has led us to colorlessness and lack of spontaneity. A little less scrupulous identity of treatment may lead to some unevenness in the offering, but it can also liberate the natural talents of young instructors and the potential exuberance of the instructed. At this stage of vigorous rethinking of our programs we do not need a voice *ex cathedra* to tell us what is the new pattern to which we must conform, thus establishing a new orthodoxy of the heterodox. We need the excitement of experimentation within our own institutions, a healthy enthusiasm for one's own brainchild, that child who flourishes despite the pessimism of those who do not recognize its hidden vitality. We need many flowers blooming, daylilies perhaps, but each in its day and hour bringing fragrance to the experience of some. Excellent teaching has always been uneven in its distribution, depending as it does on the presence or absence of gifted individuals who stand out in the memory of the instructed.

I have talked at some length about the transients. Let us consider now those who will stay in the commune and draw from it a major part of their undergraduate experience. I cannot deal here with all aspects of the undergraduate program although there is much one could say about each. Let me keep to one or two facets which are particularly close to my own interests and in serious need of development. Here I shall begin with the language program for majors and minors. It is not enough to say, ostrich-like, "Send them abroad for a year," thus saving ourselves the taxing effort of seeking solutions for some of the toughest problems with which we have to deal. The year abroad undoubtedly helps but not all can participate and in our commune the interests of all are our concern. Let us face the fact that the improvement of language skills at the so-called "advanced" level is one of the most difficult of our tasks and yet it is the area toward which the least research and inquiry have been directed.

First we must meet the student where he is. Students complain about the gap between their intermediate course (or their high school experience) and the advanced courses. How do we explain this gap? It is very real to instructors and students alike. Two folk-explanations are prevalent: "nobody has taught them anything in their earlier courses" and "the students are a feckless lot; if they really cared they wouldn't keep on making the same mistakes." If the same situation persists from year to year with successive groups of students and we know the most energetic language teaching is going into the earlier courses, perhaps the time has come to look more critically at ourselves and our courses at this level. Most of the instructors, being trained in literary scholarship, want to teach literature primarily so they proclaim loudly that they are not there to teach the language. The students, they say, should know the language already. In their anxiety to protect themselves from such an unwelcome task they conveniently forget the many years it took them to perfect their own knowledge of the language (and this applies to the native speakers among them too) and the pitifully short language programs still prevalent in this country.

Because extra language work is, however, a clear necessity, we set up some language courses and farm these out as perennial chores for less influential or more accommodating members of the department. Anyone can do it, so sometimes the task is undertaken by a young literary scholar who wants a semester with little preparation so that he can write up that article from his thesis. Few materials are available at this level so the same old book does the job. Since very few are really interested in the design of the courses the language is chopped up into unnatural and unpalatable segments—a unit of diction this semester (such terrible pronunciation!), a unit of syntax next semester, not forgetting a unit or two of composition (no one has taught them to write decently in the language, and they'll need this skill for their literary papers). Finally, we allot four hours, or even eight hours, to intensive conversation (the hardest of all to teach but fobbed off most frequently on untrained and often completely inexperienced native speakers who proceed to do all the talking for want of familiarity with techniques for eliciting speech).

Have we ever stopped to consider seriously whether language can be learned effectively in this piecemeal fashion? To learn language well one has to enjoy learning it so that one is eager to know how to express oneself more correctly or more elegantly. The many snippets of knowledge the student needs are assimilated into his functioning system only after conscious and alert attention is directed to them. Sometimes in language departments we seem to have a puritanical fear of students enjoying what is good for them.

A typical student comment quoted from the course evaluation booklet of my own institution will arouse acquiescence
from many unenthusiastic instructors shanghaied into language teaching: "No matter what the language, grammar
reviews are all the same: distasteful but good for you, sort of
the cod liver oil of language courses."[1] What we need to
consider is: can syntax be learned efficiently apart from
conversation, composition, and diction? Syntax taught in
isolation is a linguistics rather than a language course, an
important course to be sure but requiring a different content
from that served up in the usual "syntax course." Sometimes
the syntax course takes the form of a rather simplistic course
in translation, where students translate short, detached
sentences containing specific "points of grammar." This is
not conceived, however, as a serious course in translation
where the student will study the nonmatching nature of
surface structures and of syntactic representations of semantic substance. A genuine translation course would train the
student to extract the thought content from stretches of
English discourse and reexpress this in the formal structures
of another language. Here we would be teaching a specialized
craft which can become a passion. Such a course is a long
way from our little artificially constructed translation
sentences which are doing violation to language as a living,
functioning entity. Living language involves at once all of the
aspects we are now teaching separately, with the addition of
the converse element of perception.

We need, then, apprenticeship classes where living language is taught as a whole, where the seamless garment is
despotted, stretched a little here, shrunk a little there, and
worn spots are invisibly mended, but where the fabric is
preserved in its integrity. In such courses syntax is considered
as it is needed, diction as it is needed, semantic structure,
communicative competence as they are needed, but all within
the context of purposeful activity, because only then does
the language come alive. Instead of talking desperately about
something or other for four, five, eight hours a week in a

---

[1] *The Advisor* (Teacher-Course Evaluation, University of Illinois, 1970-71), p.
125.

"conversation class," the group undertakes some project together and in carrying it through uses the language, improves its use of the language, corrects its use of the language: an advanced language class, a living language class—call it what you will, it is the integrated activity which counts. A series of language courses of this type can be designed so that each will unobtrusively zero in on specific problem areas. Is it diction which is defective? The course may focus on play and poetry reading for pleasure. Is written French the problem? Activities will be designed that require the writing of a large number of letters or reports that will have some destination: perhaps in the exchange of information with a group˙outside the university; an activity may be designed in the first part of the course that must be carried out in the second half, such as the writing of a scenario for a radio drama or a film based on an incident which took place in the country where the language is spoken; the class may take over the regular writing and editing of a daily or weekly departmental newspaper. If general language practice is sought, activity or "case packets" can be designed which lead the students into simulating problem-solving situations which require them to search out information in printed sources and from native speakers on campus, to discuss their findings together, and to write some form of report for final presentation. During such activities gaps in the knowledge of syntax will continually reveal themselves, but the students will be taught to seek out the facts themselves from reference material or from the instructor as they need them, or to teach each other, rather than being subjected to the fourth, (fifth, sixth?) formal exposition of the workings of the object pronoun system. Such an activity class may well be linked to literary or cultural subjects and serve as an opportunity for students to familiarize themselves with wider areas of interest as they seek to discover how certain themes have been expressed at certain periods in literature, how certain ideas have been worked out in drama, or how certain aspects of life are experienced in another culture. Interesting content is needed for a language class. Such a class will differ from an introductory literature course, however, in that the purpose of the course will be quite frankly the perfection of language in use.

If we make available a series of courses of this type of varied interest and emphasis we can provide for the discrepancy in student needs. Four courses of this nature would not form a sequence to be taken by all in strict order: some would need all, some none; some would be interested only in the second and the fourth, others in the first or the third. Instructors could concentrate on improving and varying the offering of a course with a particular emphasis on an area in which they were most interested. But here comes the crunch. Our students, we are told, "prefer" literature classes—they are bored with language classes.

There are perhaps readily identifiable reasons why our students seem to prefer literature. Literature courses are at present taught by specialists who love their specialty; interesting, even exciting materials are readily available; professors spend much time preparing, finding supplementary materials, encouraging lively debate; students soon sense which are the "real" subjects which "count" in the department. Let us take the obverse which clearly applies: language classes for the most part are not taught by specialists who love their specialty; interesting and exciting materials are not readily available; professors teaching such courses as an imposed chore resent spending time seeking out, or preparing personally, materials which will not provide that idea for a future article and which will not be regarded as "scholarly production" when they are being considered for promotion or tenure; students soon sense that these courses are held in low esteem by fellow-students, professors, and their own instructor.

The situation will continue as it is at present until as foreign-language departments we are willing to accept the need for highly qualified, respected, imaginative, academically rewarded language specialists. I am not speaking of linguists, philologists, or phoneticians, but language teachers who know how to design materials and write materials, and who can integrate language use with intellectually stimulating, thought-provoking, exciting activity. To do this effectively they will need to have an informed knowledge of many areas, but they will be devoted specialists nevertheless. We need specialists in contemporary language and language learning who are also informed about different approaches to teaching, who can teach in teams, who can use students to teach their peers, who can help students to learn without interposing themselves in the learning process. We need specialists who understand that testing is primarily a device to encourage learning; who do not consider group work a kind of cheating, or take-home examinations, or open-ended or open-book examinations, as "lowering standards;" who can see the virtue in a student's discussing his paper freely in class and then going home to rewrite it in a final version or being permitted to retake tests to improve his grade. There are many well-attested devices for improving the quality and quantity of learning which are suspect to many of the stalwarts of the pyramid, but which will seem merely humane and fruitful in the commune, where change is not feared but welcomed when it promotes the good of the greatest number. I have called for proper recognition of language teaching specialists, but it must now be clear that such a group could be subversive, promoting a quiet revolution in our inner circles.

So that we do not create a group of initiates at odds with the rest of the commune, and so that other areas may profit from the shared spirit of innovation and renewal, we need a seminar for study and discussion where all future professors will have the opportunity to thrash out in common the problems of the total commune, where each can come to understand the preoccupations of the other, where our future professors will be shaken out of the ruts into which their own educational experience has settled them, where they will get to the roots of the educational problems facing them and acquire the flexibility to solve them that comes through knowledge and understanding of their causes. In other words, we need enlightened training for our teaching assistants, not in teaching techniques for tomorrow's class but as preparation for a long career. We need imaginative professors who will accept teaching assistants as co-workers, team members in the teaching of all kinds of courses, showing them innovative and stimulating learning situations in progress and giving them freedom to create others. This we can have in the free and unguarded, unsuspicious atmosphere of the commune as we could never expect it on our separate steps of the pyramid.

Teacher training, graduate preparation? There are many other areas which need a fresh wind blowing into the corners and through the doors of offices and classrooms. Let us establish our commune and these areas too will gradually open themselves up for intensive discussion and cooperative action.

10

Teacher - Student Relations:
Coercion or Cooperation? *

In *Teachers and the Children of Poverty*, Robert Coles
quotes a child from an urban slum who speaks of his school
experience in the following terms: "Are you trying to figure
out if school makes any difference to us, because if that's it, I
can tell you, man, here in my heart, it don't, much. You
learn a few tricks with the numbers, and how to speak like
someone different, but you forget it pretty fast when you
leave the building, and I figure everyone has to put in his
time one place or the other until he gets free...."[1] This
child is not speaking of the foreign-language class specifically,
but what he says may well express the attitudes of many of
our early foreign-language dropouts and even of those who
stay two or three years in the high school course. Harry
Reinert, in an investigation of the attitudes of students
toward foreign languages, found that "well over half of them
indicated that college requirements—either for admission or
graduation—influenced their original enrollment in foreign
language classes" and that "both by word and deed these
students showed that once they had completed these

*Reprinted from *New Teachers for New Students*, published by the Washington
Foreign Language Program, Seattle, Washington, and the American Council on the
Teaching of Foreign Languages, New York City, New York, at Seattle,
Washington, 1970.

requirements, they intended to have nothing more to do with foreign language."[2] "Traditional requirements with their standards of credit hours and grades have unfortunately developed into a system of timeserving"[3]—these words written in 1944 might well have been written in 1970. It may be that the present tendency for some foreign-language requirements to be eliminated will serve foreign-language teachers well by forcing them to examine the relevance in this late twentieth-century period of their objectives as reflected in what actually goes on in their classrooms (as opposed to the aims set out in syllabuses and in the literature), as well as their views on whom they do, and do not, welcome in their classes and the types of learning experiences they provide for their students.

The tyranny of requirements has made it possible for many a teacher to present a sterotyped, unimaginative course to his conscripted clientele. Not many students, we would hope, have had to suffer under such procedures as were employed in one advanced class in a New York high school in 1970. Most of the year was spent "reading" one French novel; for this, the class was divided into two groups, each of which prepared alternate sections. The sections were then subjected to grammatical and lexical dissection. By this method, no student officially read the whole novel or even a consecutive half of it. Such nonsensical teaching would never be endured by successive groups of students—unless they were coerced into the class by some obligation extrinsic to foreign-language study.

If foreign language is to maintain its position in the school curriculum unprotected by external requirements, we will need to convince students as well as administrators that it has a fundamental and unique contribution to make to the educational experience, a contribution which the students can perceive as relevant to their real concerns. For years, protagonists of foreign languages have made extravagant claims about the remarkable vocational value of their subject. A foreign-language major, we have said, can become a diplomat, a foreign correspondent, an executive in an international business complex, or a private secretary to a man who travels from world capital to world capital. What we have not been willing to admit is that ours is, vocationally speaking, an auxiliary study. A diplomat needs a solid background of history and political science, and, in his adolescence, the future diplomat does not know which language he will need in later life. A foreign correspondent needs to be a first-rate journalist. A company with international branches needs first of all a man with engineering training, business experience, or advertising or public relations expertise. The businessman who travels the world wants first and foremost a person who can handle competently his correspondence and reports, and keep unwelcome intruders away from his door. The student has a right to expect more from a study which is going to take a great deal of his time and energy for a number of years than a half-developed skill which he may or may not find useful at some hypothetical moment in his future career. And the administrator needs more convincing reasons than the vocational ones for continuing the foreign-language program in his school.

The unique contribution of foreign-language study that is truly educational, in the sense that it expands the student's personal experience of his environment, and truly humanistic in that it adds a new dimension to his thinking, is the opportunity it provides for breaking through monolingual and monocultural bonds. Such an experience reveals to the student that there are other ways of saying things, other values and attitudes than those to which his native language and .culture have habituated him. Through this process, he may develop new attitudes to ideas and peoples that will reduce his bondage to the familiar and the local, while increasing his sympathy for persons of other cultures and languages. The new-generation student in our schools is internationalist and interculturalist in his aspirations; he is also brutally direct in demanding the rationale of what we are doing and what we are asking him to do. This basic contribution which foreign language can make to his development is one which he would welcome, but he must see that what we do in our classrooms really achieves such a purpose or he will drop out as soon as he conveniently may. If, as

Harold Taylor has said: "The first task of education . . . is to raise the level of awareness and response to *all* ideas, events, people and objects,"[4] then foreign language, taught with this end firmly in view, can still claim that it has a rightful place in the overall educational program of the school.

Can our teachers meet the challenge of providing the genuinely mind-stretching experience of exploring other ways of thinking? Certainly teachers trained only in habit-formation techniques of skill training will find it difficult to deal with sensitive areas of attitudes and values; and teachers for whom cultural understanding means the description of picturesque costumes worn for religious festivals or the measurements of the Eiffel Tower will find it difficult to explain why students are disturbed in Berlin, in Paris, and in Tokyo. The teacher of the future will need to be well read, alert to current trends, receptive himself to ideas other than those of his own culture, and flexible enough to reexamine his own ideas at regular intervals in order to keep in touch with a new generation and a rapidly changing world. Such a teacher is not produced by a rigid teacher training program where the "right" answers and the "right" techniques are forced upon him as he is shaped and molded. Coercive training can only produce either a coercive teacher or a rebel against all that this training held to be of value. The teacher of the future needs to be given a deep understanding of the bases of what he is trying to do so that he will be able to adapt familiar techniques intelligently and develop new ones as circumstances change and new demands are made upon him. His association with those who train him must bring him to the realization that only a person of open mind, willing to consider and weigh many points of view, can develop such qualities in those who study with him.

We have paid lip service to this cultural objective for a number of years, but students and faculty do not see that any such enrichment is evident in those who have spent a year or two in our classes. They sometimes accuse us of rationalizing the irrelevance of our subject. The approach of most teachers is built on the belief that students must attain a high degree of language skill before they can really perceive and appreciate cultural differences reflected through language. Such training is, of course, important; it is our primary task and must not be neglected. We must ask ourselves, however, how we can give some part of this mind-broadening experience to every student no matter what his level of attainment in the language. It seems evident that any degree of cultural understanding will require a depth of discussion and thought which our high school students cannot cope with in the foreign language. Insistence on the exclusive use of the foreign language in the classroom and the more recent emphasis in some circles on the discouraging of questions from students in order to maintain this artificial atmosphere have meant the reduction of classroom "discussion" to trite questions and answers on the content of what is seen, heard, or read. The questions which are of real interest to the students are thus suppressed, and their misconceptions remain unidentified. Acting out roles is one way for the language student to get the feel of cultural differences, but, without some frank discussion, the learning of cultural differences must remain at the stage of such overt manifestations as greetings, festivals, or eating habits, viewed out of context and interpreted by the student according to his own culturally determined values and attitudes. The interest of the students in the foreign culture must be fostered from the beginning with research projects using any and all materials available, whether in the foreign language or not, with the encouragement of vigorous discussion at the points of contrast. Such projects need not take valuable time away from the language learning activities that should rightfully occupy the time the teacher has with his students; the projects should be given as out-of-class assignments, and class time should be taken only for discussion of the findings.

A study of two widely used Level 4 texts shows that even at this stage the questions on reading passages are still at the level of content (mere recall or identification of specific details), and are so structured that the one right answer must emerge. With this type of question, it is easy for the teacher to imagine that the whole class is alert and participating intelligently, whereas they are merely giving the teacher "the right answer and the right chatter,"[5] a thing they learn to do with equal ease in the foreign or the native language. Such practices are stultifying to intelligent students who revel in bull sessions and the discussion of controversial issues with their fellows. At the advanced stage, some discussion must be permitted in the native language if the student does not yet have the fluency to handle complex ideas. Such discussions are motivational and encourage the student to pursue more diligently the difficult goal of full control of the foreign language. In this period of open and uninhibited discussion, our students will no longer suffer one-way "communication" in which the teacher has all the advantages. The day of "the silent generation" to which many of our teachers themselves belonged has passed. Our new generation of teachers must be trained to handle discussion, to welcome expression of student opinion, to be willing to admit when they do not know the answer, and to cooperate with students in finding out the things they most want to know about the foreign people and the ways they think and react.

Having established a truly educative purpose in foreign-language study other than mere skill training, the foreign-language teacher of the seventies will have to answer the question: "Is this experience of value to all students?" It is the task of the educator to consider the needs of all youth: the gifted, the average, the less able, and, of particular emphasis at this time, the disadvantaged. For too long the foreign-language teacher has sought a privileged role in the school: only an elite of bright, alert, well-motivated students was acceptable in his class—all others were, in his view, "incapable of learning a foreign language." Sometimes the mathematics teacher, the science teacher, the history teacher, and the art teacher have felt the same way about their students, and would have preferred a select group—yet students of all levels of ability and all backgrounds still come to be taught.

The foreign-language teacher of the past found himself unable to teach any but the more intelligent and more highly motivated students because he had turned foreign language into an abstract study of grammatical forms and relationships, followed by the close analysis of modes of expression divorced from the stream of common life—classical tragedy, nineteenth-century prose—which, with his academic approach, he was unable to relate, as they may well be related, to the preoccupations and concerns of the present day. In a reversal of trends, he may have moved away more recently from a traditional presentation to one involving drills and repetitive practice of inert phrases, material which students have felt to be of little concern to them at a stage when the body of educative experience presented to them in other subjects emphasizes productive and creative thinking. Despite his initial advantage, then, the foreign-language teacher has also frequently lost the gifted students, who see foreign-language study as sterile and unrewarding.

We may ask with these students why, in most schools, they must be forced to accept a uniform foreign-language diet established by tradition or by the uncontested prestige of college professors unacquainted with, and often uninterested in, the interests and capacities of high school students. After the elementary general-purpose textbooks have been completed, who has decided that all foreign-language students, no matter what their abilities or interests, must study a series of literary "masterpieces," often of a bygone era? How frequently are such senior students allowed to participate in the selection of what they will do with their time and energies? Some may be interested in contemporary social problems, some in history, some in scientific developments, some in the arts or the everyday experiences of a foreign people, and some in the modern novel or contemporary theatre. The interests of boys may well be different from the interests of girls. Some high schools do make provision at this stage for personal choice and decision, providing resource materials for individual and group research projects in which students read, listen to, and discuss all kinds of material in the foreign language, but such progressive programs are all too few. If the final high school years provide only "more of the same," it should not surprise the foreign-language teacher when even the better students are reluctant to continue beyond the minimum requirement.

Even at earlier levels it is possible to allow students some autonomy in the selection of activities according to their personal predilections if at least some part of the program is individualized. Should we expect all students, even the inarticulate, to want to develop their speaking skills primarily? Some in this television generation, if allowed to choose, might prefer to look and listen. (Teachers should be aware of research that shows a different rate of native-language development for boys and girls, in the girls' favor; this has a cumulative effect,[6] and may affect personal preferences at a certain age). Some students may prefer to range beyond the rest of the class in reading (graded readers which cover a wide variety of topics are available in the more commonly taught languages). Such individualization of choices requires imaginative planning by a classroom teacher who is willing to go beyond a steady, uniform, universal diet for at least part of the time. An experimental study of Robert Politzer and Louis Weiss has shown that "better results were obtained by the pupils of those teachers who went beyond the procedures strictly prescribed by the curriculum, teachers who were concerned with supplementing the curriculum rather than merely implementing it." It seems that "the efficiency of the individual teacher increase(d) with the amount of his *personal* stake and *personal* contribution to the instructional processes."[7] To complete the picture, involvement in personally selected tasks is intrinsically motivating to normal students whose natural enjoyment of cognitive exploration has not been completely stifled by the formalism of an educational system which overemphasizes such extrinsic rewards as grades and promotions.[8]

Some schools have already experimented with student involvement in decision-making; at the McCluer High School, for example, teachers and students work cooperatively in "a non-graded curriculum stressing individualized learning through small group activities and team teaching."[9] More teachers will need to launch out into new instructional approaches, and teachers coming into the profession will need to be made aware of new possibilities in providing the proper environment for learning if foreign languages are to keep the interest and allegiance of a voluntary clientele.

To move down the scale of ability, not infrequently a student of very average ability becomes fascinated with foreign-language study. For him, it has provided a new beginning at a stage when an accumulation of undigested facts or principles from earlier years has given him a feeling of hopelessness in certain other subject areas. Everyone begins the foreign language at the same time, and he feels he has as much chance as his neighbor to assimilate it. Such students are often more successful with some aspects of foreign-language study than others. Sometimes a very average or less gifted student will find that he can understand anything he hears in the foreign language, but is unable to use the language actively with any fluency. The tests most teachers devise penalize this type of student severely, and, despite his high degree of motivation and undoubted skill in one area, he may find himself advised not to continue with the language. His teacher does not realize that many people are very popular because they listen appreciatively, murmuring from time to time only "Yes," "of course not," or "you're absolutely right." An individualized program will enable a student of this type, or a student who can read with ease but has inhibitions in speaking, or a student who can converse fluently but is a poor reader, to continue his study with a special emphasis in the area in which he feels most at home.

Finally, what has the foreign-language teacher to offer to the disadvantaged student? He may say: "I cannot teach the disadvantaged. They cannot learn a foreign language. Why—some of them cannot even read or write their own language with any degree of success!" Again, if foreign language does have some genuine educational value, it must surely have something to offer to those whose backgrounds have limited their horizons. It will not, however, be successful in the hands of a teacher who doubts the success of his enterprise even before it begins. Studies of students of a low socio-economic status have shown that they already suffer from a feeling of insufficiency, and readily accept the implications of defeat that the unconvinced teacher finds hard to conceal in his relations with them. The teacher expects them to fail, and they fail. If success is to be achieved in teaching foreign languages to disadvantaged students, teachers-in-training and experienced teachers alike will need to study the preoccupations, value systems, and characteristic approaches of these young people.[10] With an understanding of their preferred modes of learning, the teacher can choose materials and design lessons which will utilize these to the full.

Students of disadvantaged groups prefer the concrete to the abstract, and respond to concrete material for which they see an immediate application. They therefore enjoy learning foreign words and phrases which they can employ immediately in the context of their class or with minority group children in their neighborhood who speak the language. Since they are not motivated by deferred rewards but seek immediate gratification, the promise that they will eventually be able to use the language fluently means little, whereas actual use of the language immediately, even in simple forms, in face-to-face interaction, is motivating. They learn through activity, through seeing, hearing, touching, manipulating, and role-playing. The teacher should use: visual presentations (flash cards, drawings, films); things the students can hold, open, shut, or pass to each other; music, songs with tapes, guitars, drums, action songs, and action poems. The vocabulary used should be practical, and should deal with the objects and actions commonly used by the students. The characters and incidents presented to them in the foreign language should never appear to be "prissy" or effeminate. These students appreciate firm leadership from the teacher, and are not anxious to work in small groups in which they will need to make group decisions. Since, in their neighborhood environment, they are accustomed to learn orally rather than through the written word (which may even present them with some difficulty in their native language) reading the foreign language will not appear to be of vital importance to them.

Since disadvantaged students are motivated by concrete, clearly visible rewards, it seems appropriate that the foreign language they are to be taught should be selected with an eye to languages spoken in their home neighborhood; in this way, the practical tangible value of the foreign language becomes obvious. Alternatively, black students today have a yearning for a clear and unambiguous identity, and are seeking this identity more and more through the exploration of their lost African heritage. There is, therefore, clearly a case for the teaching of Swahili, or some other African language, in high schools, as many black groups have been demanding. Teachers of Spanish, French, and German should be foreign-language teachers first, rather than desperate defenders of hard-won fiefdoms; they should be advocates of more foreign-language learning, not of more learning only of Spanish or French or German. If we genuinely believe in the fundamental value of some foreign-language study for all students, then surely we should exploit this desire to learn a specific language among one large group of disadvantaged people. Swahili, or Arabic, or Yoruba will give students insights into how language operates just as surely as the more commonly taught languages, and will give them equal insights into other ways of thinking and other sets of cultural values.

The immediate response of many teachers will be: "But we don't have teachers of Swahili readily available." The answer is that we must acquire them. Swahili is considered one of the less difficult languages to learn in the Defense Language Institutes, and it does not have a strange script. The logical approach would appear to be to provide intensive training courses in Swahili for practicing foreign-language teachers, who could then introduce the language as a further offering of their language departments. Would not this also help some middle-class Americans to understand a completely different culture and the aspirations of a group of young nations striving to advance into modern statehood? Young teachers-in-training are sometimes invited to undertake the learning of a completely different language as one of their education courses in order to experience afresh the problems of language learning. Courses of this type could be used for giving them some basic knowledge of Swahili. It seems better for trained language teachers to take up this cause rather than leave it in the hands of linguistically unsophisticated amateurs.

This same line of reasoning should apply in areas where there is a strong concentration of immigrant groups speaking a particular language, since students learning a language for educational, rather than vocational, reasons will be more motivated if the language they are learning can be used and heard in everyday life.

Finally, the success of foreign languages in the years to come must lie with those teachers whom we are training at the present time. They will need to innovate, to experiment, to initiate new programs. We must train them to expect and to respect a new clientele. With the experience they themselves have of participation in decision-making and of planning for change, they will be much more fitted than any preceding generation to work with their students in developing new approaches, new techniques, and a new place for foreign languages in the educative process.

FOOTNOTES

[1] R. Coles, *Teachers and the Children of Poverty* (Washington, D. C.: The Potomac Institute, 1970).

[2] Harry Reinert, "Student Attitudes Toward Foreign Language—No Sale!" *Modern Language Journal*, 54(1970): 107.

[3] Otto K. Liedke, "A Historical Review of the Controversy between the Ancient and the Modern Languages in American Higher Education," *German Quarterly*, 17(1944): 1-13, reprinted in M. Newmark, *Twentieth Century Modern Language Teaching* (New York: Philosophical Library, 1948), pp. 11-21.

[4] Quoted by A. E. Lean in *And Merely Teach* (Carbondale: Southern Illinois University Press, 1968), p. 58.

[5] John Holt, *How Children Fail* (New York: Dell, 1970), p. 42. Originally published by Pitman, 1964.

[6] Dorothea A. McCarthy, "Sex Differences in Language Development" in R. G. Kuhlen and G. G. Thompson, eds., *Psychological Studies of Human Development* (New York: Appleton-Century-Crofts, 1970), pp. 349-353.

[7] R. L. Politzer and L. Weiss, "Characteristics and Behaviors of the Successful Foreign Language Teacher," Stanford Center for Research and Development in Teaching, Technical Report No. 5 (Palo Alto, April 1969), pp. 69-70.

[8] E. J. Murray, *Motivation and Emotion* (Englewood Cliffs, N.J.: Prentice-Hall, 1964), pp. 74-82.

[9]F. H. Wood, "The McCluer Plan: An Innovative Non-Graded Foreign Language Program," *Modern Language Journal*, 54(1970): 184-87.

[10]Two useful references are H. Sebald, *Adolescence: A Sociological Analysis* (New York: Appleton-Century-Crofts, 1968) and A. Shumsky, *In Search of Teaching Style* (New York: Appleton-Century-Crofts, 1968).

Index